The Leadership App:

Your Blueprint to Achieving Enduring Success in Leadership

By Will Emmons

"The Leadership App: Your Blueprint to Achieving Enduring Success in Leadership," by Will Emmons. ISBN 978-1-949756-14-2 (eBook); 978-1-949756-15-9 (Softcover); 978-1-949756-16-6 (Hardcover).

Published 2019 by Virtualbookworm.com Publishing Inc., P.O. Box 9949, College Station, TX 77842, US.

Acknowledgements

I would like to thank the many people who made this book possible. First, I would like to thank my wife and my two sons. I have spent more time on planes and in foreign countries than most people can even begin to imagine. Through it all you were supportive and understanding as I chased my dreams and fought the fight.

I would like to thank my parents. You gave me everything you had to give and taught me much of the work ethic I have to this day.

I have a special place in my heart for the people from my international teams. I would like to thank Anders, Fred, Alex, Manto, Karsten, Katherina, Henry, Premlesh, Dave, Vlad, and Brian. I loved every moment of our time together and I will always look back on our accomplishments as one of the greatest ever. Also, thank you to the countless others in sales, marketing, customer success, product, finance, and ops who were such a huge component of our success.

From my North America teams, I want to thank John, Jamie, Jason, Andy, Beth, Dennis, Brandon, Mike Z, Doug, Brian, Meghan, Tara, Tom, Brent G, Jay, Joe, Ted, Brandon, Adam, Corey, Chad, Mike C, Patrick, Janet, Miriam, and so many others. All of you impacted my life and contributed to my success.

An especially loud shout-out to my crew: Ben, Charlie, and Vinnie. You are collectively some of the most impressive business leaders I have had the privilege to work alongside.

Special thanks to Dave, Chimane, Jen, Angela, and Jackie. Leaving there was one of the hardest decisions of my life, as I loved working with you all so much.

To Farhan, I want to thank you for your trust and your friendship. I learned a ton working for and with you. I will forever look forward to our next bourbon night...whenever that might be.

Matt, thank you for showing all of us how to build a winning culture. You showed all of us what it means to respect one another, the importance of developing people, and what it means to be a true leader. Mostly, you were a constant example to all of us on how to act with dignity, respect, and with good character. You are truly unique.

Last, a very heartfelt thank you to Mark Joseph Mongilutz, who not only encouraged me to write this book, but guided me through the process as well. Mark worked in my employ years ago and is now an accomplished writer and friend.

Table of Contents

Foreword

By Jamie Crosbie, Founder and CEO of Proactivate

I'VE HAD THE GREAT PRIVILEGE in my professional life to work alongside the very best sales leaders.

Prior to launching ProActivate in 2005, I served as Vice President of Sales at CareerBuilder.com. We consistently challenged our leadership team to uphold the highest professional standards and to serve with excellence.

Among the wisest decisions I would make in my career was that of hiring Will Emmons into a sales leadership role. Will continually compelled me to grow as he exceeded all achievement metrics and elevated the organization to new heights. He not only challenged me as his leader, but demanded the best from his team and taught each team member how to maximize their own success. Will's fervent mindset allowed him to grow into executive leadership and to step comfortably into my position when I launched ProActivate.

You will learn much about sales leadership fundamentals in reading this book, but there is one thing you must also know about Will from a personal and professional perspective. Will is the most loyal person I have ever known. For that reason, among many others, the sales professionals who have benefited from Will's leadership in any capacity are changed for life, and only for the better. Will dedicates all he has to helping others be their very best and challenges them to become heroes in the eyes of their clients. More on that below.

Gerhard Gschwandtner, CEO and founder of Selling Power, once taught me that one of the single most critical characteristics of a good leader is their ability to exhibit empathy toward those they are charged with leading. That word itself, "empathy," is derived from the Greek "empatheia," meaning the ability to sense other people's emotions, coupled with the ability to imagine what someone else might be thinking or feeling. Will embodies the concept of empathy and cares passionately about his team members, both personally and professionally. He has the ability to put himself in their shoes as he leads by example in helping them reach their respective purposes with intention.

I wish this book was written when I first became a sales leader, because it is real, it is relevant, and it adopts a step-by-step approach to clearly characterizing true sales leadership, as opposed to sales management. Many in our profession are promoted into sales leadership without a clue as to what to do next. Even those who think they know don't necessarily have a leadership process. In that respect, this book more than delivers. It contains everything a sales leader needs to know and to live by in doing right by their team, and in maximizing their own professional success!

A sales professional and former Marine who sat on flight US 1549—which was piloted by "Sully" Sullenberger and crash-landed in the Hudson River shortly after takeoff from LaGuardia Airport—once shared with a mentor of mine the following words: "Everyone on the plane was quiet. Not one person panicked. As a Marine, I was trained to focus on one mission at a time. I said my prayers and when we landed I helped people get into the lifeboat." He lifted five people out of the ice-cold water and helped them climb the 12-foot ladder up to the rescue boat, with Captain Sullenberger climbing up last.

There are many heroes in this world; as a sales leader, your role is to transform your salespeople into heroes. Will relentlessly strives to achieve that goal and is consistently successful in doing so. His book will surely guide you and others to his level of leadership excellence.

Happy Leading,
Jamie

Introduction

A GOOD FRIEND OF MINE would often remind me that offering advice amounts to a shallow act. He constantly worked to lead by sharing real life stories. Imagine asking someone who has never defused a bomb whether to cut the red or the blue wire. You might appreciate hearing an outside opinion, but accepting input from someone who has, you know, *defused bombs in the past* would be ideal!

I have come to embrace this philosophy over the years when asked for advice on matters as simple as color choices, as touchy as difficult marriage advice, and as situationally specific as important business questions. If I can draw on experiences from my own past, ones I feel are relevant to the decision-making process, I'll share them. If I cannot, I simply reply, "Having never been through that before, it's hard for me to offer you advice.".

What most people are looking for when requesting advice is validation that the decision they think is right is, in fact, right...based on *their own* experiences (limited though they might be). Offering a different point of view without merit or experience diminishes the legitimacy of that advice and simply creates more doubt. However, if you *have* experienced the same problem and came out the other side with a positive result (or at least lived to tell about it), there may well be value in whatever it is you have to say.

When writing this book, I tried to base my every leadership prescription on a compilation of personal experiences. Much of what I have to share is based on mistakes I have made; much is based on things that went well the first time around. But most of what I have shared could be categorized as techniques which have been tested, re-tested, fine-tuned, rinsed, washed, and repeated over and over again, and with high levels of success.

My hope is that the reader will enjoy those stories I have interwoven with the lessons herein. I have had the pleasure of working with some amazing people over the years. Some worked with me, many for me, and others over me. I can honestly say I learned from all of them. Some were tremendous examples of how *not* to lead—I have had a handful of those over the years! Others left me with some leadership/sales best practices. Some were my guinea pigs (sorry about that), and others brightly validated the strength of my process.

I once asked a leader of mine how he knew so much information. He simply pointed to a box in the corner of his office filled with books and explained that almost everything I might want to know has been written about by someone. You just have to invest the time to seek that knowledge. So, I started reading a lot of business books. That was over twenty years ago. What I generally found in many of those books was an interesting concept or theme populating the first three chapters, which then trailed off or vanished entirely as I continued reading.

My goal with this book was to provide cover-to-cover value. I hope to have succeeded in that goal.

Also, one of my core beliefs: If I can learn from the mistakes of others, I will take that path to success, rather than a path riddled with endless errors. Keeping that in mind, I really worked to be as transparent as possible and to display for you both my failures along the way, and the successes to which they contributed.

Last, this is a book on leadership. Many of the references I make are sales-centric, due mostly to the fact that most of my time was spent in that arena. However, know that the lessons within are easily transferable to virtually any category of business.

While it is far from over, I have truly treasured my career so far. I have had the fortune of running some incredible businesses all over the world. I have been honored to meet some extraordinary people and have led some great individuals along the way. I would like to express my thanks to all of you who have been a part of my leadership journey—Thank you for your friendship and support.

-Will Emmons

Chapter I:
My Journey to Date... and
the Road Ahead

GOING STRICTLY BY DATE OF BIRTH, my story begins in 1973. But this book isn't about my story, at least not entirely. It is a book about my philosophy on business, on leadership, and on life. Like most of us, many of the attributes I embrace today were shaped early in my life. By and large, *that* story begins in the early 1980s, and with the recession which impacted the United States during that period.

I don't know how the recession of that time period affected other families, but it hit our family especially hard. Making matters worse was the fact that my father, despite his willingness to labor through thick and thin, couldn't seem to find either thick or thin for an extended period in that time. That's one of the great tragedies of possessing a strong work ethic: When there is no work to be done, that ethic exists in a vacuum. Unemployment brought on by the closing of a plant tends to yield that result.

By my measure, my father was a hero in more ways than one. Drafted into the Vietnam War halfway through college, his life was uprooted and forever changed as a result. While in the war, he met and married my mother; upon returning, they quickly started a family. My parents did everything in their power to make ends meet, and eventually my father worked his way back through school. He did so while providing as best he could and taking care of what would eventually total three children (with me in the middle). I started my own family later in life, which meant I had the luxury of taking risks, of pursuing better opportunities. My father had no such luxury—his considerable energies were spent trying to put food on the table. As you might imagine, there were times when this proved more difficult than any of us would have hoped.

My mom did her part to keep food on the table as well, and at times it took everything both of them had to meet the needs of the family, but they did it...make no mistake. My mom was not only hard-working, but proud. I remember when things got especially tough on us, my uncle sent a check in the mail to try and help make ends meet. Mom, while she greatly appreciated, was not having it. With tears in her eyes, she put the check right back in the mail. She was determined to survive this difficult time on her own two feet.

This is not a plea for pity; keep your pity. I don't need it, haven't asked for it, and wouldn't benefit in the slightest from it. Not in the 1980s, not now.

No, this is not a sympathy grab. It is an explanation as to why I approach business in the way that I do.

You see, financial struggles of the sort I witnessed seem to have one of two effects on people: 1. It traps a person in its clutches and imprisons them in a self-defeating mindset forever, or 2. It compels them to escape its grasp and never look back. Ever.

I'll give you three guesses as to which effect took root in my mind. I made a promise to myself even back then. I declared that:

"I will do whatever it takes to ensure I never put my own family in that situation."

And so, I began my quest.

As far back as my elementary school years, I had a paper route. The job was pure, provided me with a sense of purpose, taught me a bit about money, and instilled in me a "come rain or shine" work ethic which accompanies me to this day. There was a palpable sense of gratification in visiting every house on my route and collecting the money owed. I was scarcely out of the single-digit age range, yet I regularly found myself participating in dozens of business transactions with neighbors who trusted and respected me.

It was a feeling I would come to appreciate greatly.

Not long after, during middle and high school, I became familiar with the concept of outsourcing. It turns out that not everybody in Texas has the time or capability to maintain their own lawn. It also turned out, in the late 1980s, that a hungry kid with strong drive and common sense to spare had plenty of time to care for lawns other than his own. After perfecting what may have been my first real sales pitch, I took my skills on the road and lined up a respectable roster of neighborhood clients.

Mowing lawns—good exercise, decent money, practical business experience. I'd say mine was a youth mostly well spent, all things considered.

But it was the minor leagues in comparison to what came next. It might go without saying by this point in the book, but mine were far from ordinary college years. Even with what I had earned and saved throughout my adolescence, money was a challenge as I worked toward my degree.

Labor wages amount to a crude but consistent calculation in the American economy. Maybe in *any* economy. The worse the job, the more someone is willing to pay to have it done. This is why roofers tend to earn more per hour than cashiers. Even if you'd like to argue that both are undesirable professions, roofing trumps cashiering. I should know—I spent time as a roofer for the simple reason that I needed to earn more per hour than what a typical college job pays. And because I thought it best to experience a broad range of crappy jobs, I also painted houses and worked as a waiter. The last of these only lasted for 24 hours. I had developed quite a chip on my shoulder, so on my first night I had a real jerk for a customer. He ended up with a plate of food in his lap and I went back to doing crappy jobs.

Eventually, ambition and a good idea took me by the bootstraps, and things were never quite the same. During our sophomore year, my roommate (the true entrepreneur) and I started our own business. You might be wondering if the business had anything to do with delivering papers, mowing lawns, roofing houses, or trying to upsell customers on premium drinks and appetizers.

It had nothing to do with any of these.

We had instead gone into the home security and home theater business. I was on a path toward sales and business success I could not have imagined ten years earlier. It could probably be said that I have been moving steadily upward ever since.

But first, there were many long days and even longer nights ahead of us. Those might have sucked at the time, but looking back now, I can't say with certainty that I would not have traded them for anything in the world. The company consisted of exactly two people, which meant strategy, sales, and labor all fell to me and to my roommate...er, I mean business partner. Did I mention we were also in school? Predictably, my grades endured a downturn as business enjoyed an upturn.

And it did pick up. Through sheer force of will (pardon the pun) and marketing cleverness, we took on as many clients as we could handle. Maybe one or two more.

Here's how we did it.

My roommate designed a logo and bought a magnetic sign to showcase it. That took care of our branding and company presence. We hired an answering service with the threefold aim of 1. handling our inbound calls, 2. providing us with a shipping address, and 3. slapping a veneer of legitimacy upon our fledgling outfit. The last of these was arguably the most important.

Above all, we worked ourselves to the bone.

Our clients were homebuilders. Which is to say, we were pitching to no-nonsense types with little time to spare. They're also a skeptical bunch and had good reason to wonder if we were up to the task. And at the risk of seeming a tad dramatic, whatever and wherever I have sold before or since, those were challenging days and served to ready me for tough sales meetings years and decades later.

It was class by day, sales by *later* day, wiring of the houses by night, and back to school the following morning. This might seem like an impossible or, at very best, *ill-advised* way to move through one's college years. Maybe it was. But I had sworn during those miserable recession years that I would never allow anyone else to determine my earning potential. Money would not be a problem for me, because I had no objections to doing what it took to make it. And I certainly didn't have any objections to inventing miniature economies of my own in order to ensure I was never without employment.

Still, I had committed myself to completing college and would unquestionably see that through. My roommate was operating under no such commitment and had dropped out by the time I was entering my senior year. His is a different kind of success story. That tiny operation we set ourselves to keeping afloat (to pay for tuition) became the bedrock of my friend's career. It is still in operation under his leadership and is among the largest privately held companies of its kind in Texas. My friend later returned to college and finished his business degree; but that, along with the story of the still-thriving business, is probably a book all its own. While I was part of that company in its early years, it was my former roommate and current friend who was the real entrepreneur. He masterminded the idea. He risked it all to keep it going in the most difficult of times. He is the success story there. Not me.

My journey with that company ended for a short time while I set out to make an even bigger splash elsewhere (a decision I still, on occasion, regret). Fate or circumstance brought me back into the company's orbit for some time in 1996. Though my partner was a dynamo on the operations side, he needed revenue, as all businesses do. As it happens, I am excellent at driving revenue. Our combined talents (deadly, that combination) had us exceeding our ability to keep pace with demand. A small fleet of company trucks, a handful of employees, and plenty of projects to fulfill—it was success of the sort we had envisioned since our sophomore year of college, even if it did come at the price of a headache now and again.

The second stint with that company was my final. In 1997, I decided to test my mettle and my sales ability in the big leagues. Like an itch I just couldn't seem to scratch, the need to *do, have,* and *be* more continued to drive me forward career-wise. Above all, the need to be respected was a compelling force in my mind. Now, twenty years later, I often allow myself to believe that aspect of my personality is under control. Often, not always.

In my youth, I imagined the vague and amorphous term "Corporate America" comprised the metaphorical salesmanship "big leagues." What that would ultimately mean for my immediate career prospects, however, was anybody's guess.

Until it wasn't.

I first entered the leviathan that is Corporate America by way of selling temporary administrators in the staffing world. It was during this time that fortune smiled upon me and my ambition, as I met a man who imparted upon me countless lessons pertinent to our business, all of them useful. He also laid down a solid foundation for sales within that space.

This was enormous.

After all, my sales acumen had been well-honed during high school and college, but the selling process in a human capital operation amounted to a different sort of rodeo. What my sales leader taught me would prove essential in the days ahead.

Time inevitably came for me to seize the next rung on the ladder, which ended up being a technology staffing group. Recognized as a strong performer in my previous role, I had also interviewed well and was granted a wholly new position within the division. Many of those with whom I worked during this time forced me to elevate my skillset once more. One in particular was, in hindsight, as much of a blessing as he was a curse. Though he had a gift for salesmanship, his character was sorely lacking in many ways.

Nevertheless, I took from our interactions what I could. That year I achieved the accolade of Number One Biller. I chose to follow the mixed blessing of a man to Colorado, where we were charged with setting up and managing offices in Boulder, Denver, and Colorado Springs. That first year, two of those offices that I launched had ascended in the ranks to hold, respectively, the number three and number five worldwide rankings.

Oddly enough, the success I had achieved would result in my being assigned the unofficial role of "corporate snitch." In other words, I was sent to struggling offices with the mission of reporting (in very close detail) on my findings. The position was hardly my calling in life, but the diagnostic aspect served me well later in my career. A cornerstone of the role was identifying shortcomings and then generating solutions to overcome them. It was snitch work on its face, but I was learning a good deal about what does and does not work in a sales environment.

I was also flying every which way around the country, often six days each week. The travel proved burdensome and was soon compounded by the fact that I had met the woman who would become my wife. Our desire to spend more time together led to my leaving that job behind, and also to a realization that I really did want to start a company of my own...eventually.

Since first dipping my toe into the world of corporate America, I have gone on to lead successful sales teams across almost every market in the United States. I have led both sales and operations in multiple countries throughout Asia, Europe, and the Middle East. I have started sales and operations teams from nothing. I have turned around sales and operations teams in steady decline. I have taken successful sales and operations teams and made them more successful. I have led single locations, regions, countries, and continents. I have enjoyed much success, but none of it came easy. It was all a result of extreme dedication to a process that I have come to know as my own. What follows is my attempt to share this with you.

There it is—my "earn the right," if you will. This book is not an autobiography, and it is not a work of self-celebration. And, as mentioned earlier, it is not a treatise on the intrinsic blessings of a poor upbringing, as a friend of mine might put it.

But I wouldn't expect you or anyone to put much stock in the chapters to come without some understanding of the life experience backing their authorship. Struggle characterized my youth, hard work my early adulthood, and leadership my nearly every year since. Between the three, I have developed a way of training and motivating sales teams and individuals which I feel can be successfully exported across the breadth of, yes, Corporate America. That once-monolithic landscape is now a playground I've come to know well.

There's a lot to cover in these pages. Eighteen years of successful leadership experience distilled into a few hundred pages. Believe it or not, for as much as we're going to touch on, quite a bit will be hitting the cutting room floor. Only the very best of what I can offer will make the final draft. Speaking of which, here are a few lessons I've learned, some of which we will be re-visiting later.

1.   Bluntness and candor are often mistaken for one another, as the terms are seen as being directly synonymous. Where the former is destructive and tends to erode both trust and confidence, the latter contributes to greater trust between leaders and subordinates while yielding clarity and allowing for meaningful growth. Do with that distinction what you will.

2.   Assumption is, for better or worse, a central part of the human experience. When you commit to attending a lunch engagement, you are necessarily (and most often correctly) *assuming* that your means of transportation will be in good working order, that you will not fall victim to a traffic delay, that the restaurant will not be closed down for a health violation, and that a snowstorm will not befall downtown Dallas in the dead of summer. Now, these are mostly safe assumptions...but they are still assumptions. In order to plan at all for the future, we must be willing to take at least a few things for granted. Without it, planning can rarely proceed.Now, having acknowledged that, I will state here that many of my most avoidable professional mistakes have been directly attributable to an over-reliance upon assumption.

The dials, I assumed, were being made. Upon inspection, it turned out they were not.

A senior sales professional, I assumed, must surely know how to run a sales meeting. After all, she came to us with seven years of experience. **The assumption**: That *all* sales experience is transferrable from one industry to another. **The fact**: It is not.

Allow assumption its due (snow will likely not hit Dallas in July), but assume nothing in a sales environment. There are too many variables, too many unknowns. Confirm early and often.

3. Added to this maxim should be a companion rule: Inspect everything. Inspect Outlook and Salesforce; inspect dial reports and service agreements; inspect travel itineraries and account reviews. Inspect as though the health of your business depends upon it, for the simple reason that it does.

4. Keep yourself informed, educated, knowledgeable. These days, there is simply no excuse to be anything but. All of recorded human history is accessible to virtually any person with a modern mobile telephone. Our ability to collect, organize, and report on client/consumer data is unprecedented. Information that the advertising titans of Madison Avenue would have bled for fifty years ago is now available to any business professional willing to look for it.

And don't forget to enhance your knowledge with adequate *context*. A 360-degree perspective is key to understanding how best your data might be leveraged, as convincingly argued in John C. Maxwell's *The 360 Degree Leader*. This means gleaning information from multiple sources. In my case, this has often meant hearing from technology, marketing, customer service, and finance experts before feeling as though my picture is complete. Potential sources will vary from industry to industry, but the principle is the same: A plurality of perspectives creates a fuller understanding of the data in play.

5.   Instinct is a powerful phenomenon. Long before humans could speak or write, we *felt* the world around us and developed a capacity for detecting danger, for sensing when things weren't as they should be, for anticipating a change of one sort or another. Long before we had the words for the sensation, we knew when a situation seemed wrong.

Trust your instincts.

In at least a handful of instances, I have made hires despite a feeling of uncertainty. Without exception, my feelings on the matter proved correct...eventually. It cuts both ways. A few hires I have made were questionable to others, as the individuals perhaps lacked the ideal resume or specific professional experience to make them an obvious fit. Again, my instincts identified something useful and worthwhile behind the resume. One of those hires had been a school teacher, a woman with seemingly no place in corporate sales. She went on to become an enormous success. Another was a zipper salesman (seriously) whose capacity for selling in the human capital industry was completely untested. He also went on to wildly exceed expectations.

Put faith in your gut feelings.

6.   My path to leadership was neither predictable nor common. I came into my own as a leader by proving myself as a teacher. Of course, my entrepreneurial endeavors in high school and

college had stoked within me the flames of independence, and the leading of others carried with it the promise of autonomy, which aligned nicely with my personality. Still, it was not naked ambition and relentless ladder-climbing that catapulted me into the captain's chair. Instead, it was my sincere love for educating others that would see me through from promotion to promotion.

Teaching people the art and the science of selling was, for me, a calling.

The reasoning was simple: I sincerely wanted my protégés to succeed. Often more so than they wanted to succeed themselves. What better impetus for teaching could one hope for? Helping others thrive became an enormous source of pride and is an aspect of leadership very much with me still. *That's* the real lesson here. If you can hitch your leadership ambitions to something noble and intrinsically valuable, the promotion process will materialize organically, intuitively, respectably.

7.   The human experience pre-dates political boundaries by innumerable centuries. Which is to say, certain behaviors and practices do not differ so greatly from country to country, at least not in business. At the end of the day, we are, all of us, very much what Desmond Morris described as "the naked ape."

An abiding reality exists within that larger truth: Business principles are not country-specific. This I can attest to after having led organizations in over twenty countries across three continents (North America, Asia, and Europe). A few observations...

No matter where I've traveled, I seem to hear arguments along the lines of "That will never work here," or "That's not how we do things." The bottom line is that business principles are applicable everywhere.

People are still driven by a desire to do good work.

Accountability is a priority no matter the country, culture, et cetera.

There is no getting around the importance of a strong value proposition.

Development of one's human capital is key.

What most certainly *is* country-specific is the particular ways in which business is conducted. Every society is governed by distinctive cultural norms which dictate how communication should take shape. The exhibiting of respect, the structuring of business deals, the scheduling and oversight of negotiations—all of these are subject to societal pressures and national customs which are inherently unique from country to country; from region to region.

This does not run contrary to my earlier point regarding business principles and their universality. In fact, it only renders that point more relevant. Underlying principles persist throughout human experience, despite enormous socio-cultural chasms. It is indeed remarkable.

But we're ahead of ourselves and will re-visit the transnational topic at greater length a few chapters hence.

8.   Your team might be comprised of the best people in the world, but absent suitable focus, that group will likely never reach its full potential. Focus allows you to win, even when burdened with inferior products or services. Conversely, you may have the greatest products in the world, but lacking necessary

focus you will almost certainly leave money on the table...lots of it. Many successful organizations have mastered this art with overlay strategies for sales people. Others fail miserably by asking one person to sell fifteen totally distinctive products. Ask one person to sell everything and they will *choose what they want to sell.* This is sometimes driven by one's compensation plan, but is more often determined by following the path of least resistance. This is arguably sustainable if you have **easy products to sell**; but one thing I know with certainty is that if you force someone to eat by doing a single difficult task, they will figure it out, and in doing so will become lean and perform efficiently. Provide them a smorgasbord from which to eat, and they will grow fat, lazy, and inefficient.

9.   Alignment is the most critical component of any winning leadership model. Alignment is the ability to communicate a plan, ensuring that everyone understands the path forward and is properly paired with their respective function in the larger effort. Remember: understanding does not necessarily imply agreement. If there is disagreement, then the plan will not be properly executed. For that reason, you must have established rules for proper engagement. I communicate the plan, you get to express your doubts/concerns, we discuss those concerns and vet them out. But at the end of the day, a decision is made (usually by the senior leader) and everyone accordingly executes. In the absence of alignment, time is wasted and plans too often fail. You must inspect alignment always, at all levels, and with extreme rigor. The moment alignment fails, the plan in its entirety will follow suit.

Okay, then—nine lessons will do for our purposes. As noted, a number of these topics will show up in subsequent pages. For now, let's wrap up my extended "earn the right" with a useful summation. I bring over two decades of sales experience to this ongoing conversation, the overwhelming majority of which has seen me operating in a leadership capacity. And though I've had many occasions to rest on my laurels, I can't bring myself to do so. My mindset is one of continual learning, of remaining mentally sharp, of imparting my knowledge upon others.

Leadership came to me intuitively and is a cornerstone of my identity. In large part, this is because I love it. I love the people I work with, I love the hunt, I love the kill. I also love earning money; if I can do those things while repairing broken systems, that's all the better. It's unlikely I'll ever retire, at least not fully. I cannot come to peace with the idea of parting ways with a way of life that has been so good to me.

This book is an exercise in broadening my reach as teacher and mentor. My hope is that others destined for careers in leadership will benefit from what I am looking to share, and that they will come to know and cherish the sensation of helping others reach their own potential.

Chapter II:
Fundamental Belief in
Leadership

As I MENTIONED IN THE FIRST CHAPTER, I once hired a zipper salesman. It was perhaps as much an act of sheer curiosity as anything else, though I did recognize talent and drive in the guy. Unsurprisingly, there was a bit of a learning curve to overcome. He was ambitious, yes, but this led him to overplay his hand at times. As I was still learning the art of leadership myself, I often elected to take the reins during joint sales meetings. After all, my job was to drive revenue for the office and for the company, wasn't it?

No. Well, yes. But also no.

My job was to develop this employee to become independent and productive, in case I got hit by a bus and died the following day—that is a leader's job.

Any short-term gains secured by my closing business for the kid were diminished by the long-term likelihood of his being incapable of closing business for himself.

To his credit, the former zipper salesman called me on this, but did so in aggressive fashion.

"Why are you always taking over when I'm trying to close deals with *my* clients?"

Now, I probably realized in that moment that he was, indeed, right. But I also realized that he was, indeed, unready to handle complex negotiations and multi-faceted deal-cutting.

"All right, I'll tell you what—the next sales meeting we take together, the floor is yours. I won't say a word."

"Good," was the strident response.

And that was that. Soon thereafter we found ourselves seated in the office of a sizable prospect (a "zero-biller," as we called them). The meeting was going rather well at first.

And then it wasn't.

On the turn of a dime, things went south. When confronted by the client with a sidewinder of a question for which no obvious answer came to mind, guess who the former zipper salesman turned to? If you guessed Will Emmons, congratulations—you've been paying attention.

But can you guess how I responded?

If you guessed that I did anything other than keep my mouth closed, you might not have been paying *close* attention.

That is, in fact, what I did. The beleaguered kid had asked that I allow him to lead his own sales meeting, and I had obliged.

The lesson cut both ways. My former zipper salesman realized that he needed to better educate himself on an industry that had absolutely nothing to do with metallic teeth sewn into various pieces of apparel. I learned that I needed to better prepare my team to function autonomously, knowledgeably, competently, and confidently.

It was an expensive pair of lessons, and we never did earn that client's business

~~~

This chapter is as much a collection of thoughts pertinent to the book's subject as a focused block of text aimed at providing you with a ten-thousand-foot view of the sales leadership landscape. For your benefit and mine, I have avoided the stream of consciousness writing approach, though I am intent on sharing my knowledge early and often. Regard this material as my philosophical lexicon and take from it what you need to engage closely with the chapters to come.

There is a saying of unknown attribution that goes like this: "A teacher is like a candle—it consumes itself to light the way for others." Now, it seems unlikely that the person responsible for those words had sales leadership in mind when first voicing them. Which is not to say that they don't apply. In fact, they align closely with my own leadership philosophy, which can be summed up even more succinctly: "It's not about you anymore."

By the way, I should stop here to offer my congratulations. If you are reading this book, it's likely because you 1. are considering a move into leadership, 2. have been promoted into a leadership role, or 3. have held a leadership role for some time and, like most good leaders, are intent on further developing your leadership ability.

No matter the specific reason, my previously stated philosophy stands. That's right, my friend, it is no longer about you. Your job is to be that candle, and to light the way for those you are charged with leading. Regardless of which category of reader/leader you fall into, this book provides a wealth of practical and easily implemented measures to improve your leadership quality and to subsequently enjoy success in your current or future role.

One thing I've reliably observed throughout my many years in the business world is that new/young leaders often struggle to understand the necessity of this shift in mindset; the shift from inward-looking ambition to outward-facing guidance. It stands to reason that many of you were, or soon will be, promoted based on your individual career achievements.

Terrific. My hat's off to you. I hope you set aside a bit of cash on the way up. Because, well, you never know.

But those achievements of which you are rightly proud were rungs on a ladder, not laurels on which to rest. Though, if you are content to rest upon them, please do so. But I also advise that you decline any promotions to a leadership position. Those positions are demanding in terms of time and energy, and your subordinates are unlikely to care about your "Sales Rep of the Quarter" placard dating back to the Bush Administration. They care about your ability to guide them as they step into the light, and you step out of it.

And they *should*. Didn't *you?*

Leadership is a necessarily selfless phenomenon. Those who undertake its responsibilities for the right reasons will find that their own success drips off the vine like a well-tended crop. You take care of your people, you develop them well, you pave for them a viable path; you do these things and your own quality will be apparent to those who matter...to those who know *what* matters in the first place.

Pause and reflect on that for a moment.

Okay, we're ready to break this concept down still further.

In business, professional autonomy is an essential, but commonly overlooked, element. The fact that you are reading this book at all suggests a level of independence that would have your own leaders, past and present, beaming with pride. But what I am referring to is the autonomy of those who look to you for guidance, knowledge, and mentoring (i.e., the components of leadership).

Where and how does this tie in to the chapter's central theme?

Glad you asked.

A core responsibility for any sales leader is the development of strong and productive salespeople who are capable of operating independently (remember the zipper salesperson). Keep in mind, many salespeople are thrilled when the boss is away and will take full advantage of such an absence. Working when a leader is not around and possessing the capacity to work effectively without being hand-held are different concepts entirely. Engendering the latter is an art form, and one you must work actively to foster within yourself.

But what does it mean to develop strong, productive, and independent salespeople?

~~~

Here's where the concept becomes a bit less intuitive than you might have imagined. What I am advising you to do is to construct reliable, tested, and adaptable *processes* that can be fulfilled by your subordinates under any circumstances. It goes beyond merely throwing your mentees to the wolves and making offerings to the business gods in hopes that a few will survive the trial. It is the envisioning and constructing of a sales engine that can be operated as effectively in your absence as it can with you at the helm.

As tired as the "What if you were hit by a bus tomorrow?" thought experiment may seem, it is one worth bearing in mind. Where a leader lacking in the way of process implementation would have to acknowledge that their team would flounder in their absence, a stronger leader who had devoted time and energy to such a project could take comfort in knowing their team would thrive regardless.

It might not be true of you, but many leaders seem to struggle with the transition from sales professional or business unit contributor to sales/team/unit/division leader.

The reasoning has everything to do with why they were promoted in the first place. For the most part, a person in any field or industry will be selected for promotion because of their superior work ethic, knowledge, interpersonal skills, or (in the sales realm) closing ability.

In other words, they tend to be the best and brightest. Their dominant and most defining characteristics are not easily switched off or repurposed.

Furthermore, an assumption tends to accompany the recently promoted into their new role. New leaders often assume that the qualities which animate their own professional energies are universal. They will proceed to offer direction and guidance with the expectation that every team member possesses a level of competence and drive equal to their own.

This is very rarely the case.

Obviously, your team members may house considerable potential within themselves. That is not in question. However, they may not yet have learned to shape and summon that potential as you have. Or, more likely, they may not have operated within a proper development structure; may not have benefited from following the steps of a thoughtfully crafted process. As a leader, you must quickly identify potential, both where it exists and where it doesn't. You must craft your processes and drill your team in their proper application(s). You must resist the temptation to treat team members like direct embodiments of your own qualities. And you must endlessly seek new opportunities to develop talent and cultivate independence.

~~~

All right, bear with me. I've been wanting to put those words in print for years. It's just that I've been so consumed with living them that the writing process took backburner status for longer than expected.

~~~

Now then, let's pivot a bit. I've provided a primer as to how newly promoted leaders should approach their role, and I'll stand by it in perpetuity. But the overriding responsibility by which every sales leader's actions and decisions should be governed is that of seeing to the success of the company. Whether hired in an entry-level capacity or brought into senior management from the start, every employee is charged with contributing to the near and long-term success of the company. Whether it is sales driving revenue, development driving product, IT driving efficiencies, marketing driving brand awareness, or finance seeing to it that the company maximizes EBITDA, every department does its part to forcefully move the organization forward.

As it happens, seeing to the success of your team members will directly contribute to the successful fulfillment of this responsibility. Honestly, it will. If they win, you win; if you win, the company wins. If the company wins...well, we could go around in circles on this, but you get the point.

Bear in mind, this reality carries with it the potential for a reversal of priorities. Many young and inexperienced leaders assume an almost parental level of protectiveness for their people, and too often at the expense of the larger organization. Without exception, the company (your employer) and its shareholders must take precedence within the framework of your decision-making process. Any professional crossroad you reach should be evaluated within a single context: Which route will serve the company and, by extension, the greater good? Once the answer to that question becomes apparent, your responsibility is to act in accordance with the company's interests.

There will be times when shielding your people from the negative consequences of their shortcomings will seem like the best course of action. It almost never is. Remember: Your people are functionaries in the larger machine of the company. Their *earned* success is essential to the company's *sustained* success.

Lastly on this sub-topic is your responsibility to the customer. I am tempted to use a juggling metaphor in describing the work of seeing to your company's needs, to your employee's needs, and to your customer's needs, but that metaphor is not quite apt. Instead, I would ask that you imagine a set of three dangling carnival rings swaying back and forth in front of a bullseye. Your job is to ensure the rings are in perfect (or near-perfect) alignment before pulling that trigger. When the round strikes home, having passed through each aperture without so much as grazing the side of any ring, you know your aim is true.

The rings—
Do right by your customer (service, pricing, quality), take care of your employees (compensation, development, credit), and see to the health of your company (revenue, invoicing and profitability). And, above all, know that the last of these is the foremost of these.

Compensation, Development, and Deal Credit

We will cover development in detail throughout this book, so let's focus on the other important factors where dealing with employees is concerned.

For our purposes, let's take these out of order and look at the example of compensation (in sales, always a balancing act). Leaders who place people above the company are prone to erring when it comes to compensation and deal credit. My philosophy on sales credit (or non-sales bonuses) and compensation dictates that your people should be paid 100% of every penny owed them; not one penny less and not one penny more. When adhered to honestly and in alignment with what they have *actually sold*, this philosophy is manageable and practical. However, when paying a rep on a deal whose closing they had nothing to do with, absolutely nobody benefits. At least not in the long run. Short-term, you'll have a happy rep who is oblivious to the fact that their sales prowess has likely been stunted by an unearned bonus.

The temptation for exceptions is ever-present in the minds of most leaders, regardless of the industry or profession. In sales, that temptation manifests in the form of manipulating numbers to provide awards and elevated compensation for those who are prone to falling *just* short of their goal(s).

Let's use a simple thought experiment to illustrate this point: Your company has a yearly awards trip which requires each Account Executive to achieve no less than 100% of their quota to be eligible. One of your AEs falls short of their number by about 1% of their total number, despite having given the year their very best effort. If you are even remotely human, your instincts will tell you to make an exception. I've certainly been tempted once or twice.

But my own humanity aside, the fact is that you really cannot give in to that urge. If you do give in, you will undoubtedly end up being asked to make exceptions all the way down the sales roster. First it was 1%, next it will 2.5%, 4%, and, before you know it, overlooking a 10% shortfall won't seem too outlandish. Where would it eventually end? What arbitrary number would be your cutoff point? Something around 12.7%, perhaps? I have a better suggestion: The number is the number. By which I mean 100% is 100%.

We should bear in mind that (most) people try their hardest. Overlooking that fact can lead to major problems with morale. Rather than acknowledge this by cheapening the meaning of 100%, find other ways to reward hard workers who occasionally have a bad quarter. Team outings, lunch on your dime, recognition—anything other than diminishing the meaning of a hard and fast quota.

Furthermore, making exceptions tends to send unintended messages. Most cripplingly, when exceptions are made, it indicates that a job as outlined in an employment contract is for some reason not doable. If your team believes for any reason that making the awards trip is not achievable without help from above (so to speak), they will embrace a mentality of defeat before the race is even underway. This is not sustainable for you, for the team, for the company.

By the way, do you absolutely despise gossip? I certainly do. I can understand it, of course, but it annoys me more than anything else. A surefire way to invite gossip upon yourself and your office is to make a quota exception. The charge of "playing favorites" is certain to follow immediately. Avoid exceptions and eliminate the gossip. Well, some of it, anyway; there will always be rumors about something or other.

Okay, now you know what *not* to do in that regard. What you *should* do, however, is ensure that closed business is being tracked accurately. Nothing less than full credit is acceptable here. If you think a few quota exceptions can damage morale, try allowing a rep to be shortchanged financially because of some bureaucratic misstep. A company I once worked for was troubled by routine crediting errors when processing payments, contracts, et cetera. If not for my steadfast philosophy (not a penny more, not a penny less), several of my people would have been victim to a department that didn't know the first thing about a hard-won sale. Perhaps more than any other behaviors I exhibited while leading for that organization, this stubbornness on my part was responsible for the enormous support and loyalty which characterized my team's regard for me. They knew that, above all, I would always fight for accurate compensation.

Pause for a moment and reflect on what you've just read. Fighting for something good and worthwhile is one of the more intuitive actions a good leader will undertake. You may ruffle a feather here and there—I say, ruffle away. Your reps and leaders being paid correctly is too important to overlook.

If you successfully navigate the landmines of compensation, credit, and recognition, you are one-third of the way there. The next areas to address are those things that allow for long-term success. These include multiple areas of focus, but as a leader, I believe the three most critical areas are driving revenue, controlling costs, and delivering positive EBITDA growth.

These items are not siloed. They are critical considerations for all areas of an organization.

Sales is the obvious source of revenue, but most functions in the organization touch that piece of the pie in some way, including customer service, account retention teams, product development teams, marketing teams, IT, and finance. These departments share the responsibility of achieving their specific charters without adding unnecessary costs. This requires diligence, self-management, and large-scope thinking.

Early in my career, I asked someone if there was a price or deal size we didn't want due to its being less/unprofitable. The response: "You are not paid on profitability, so don't worry about profitability.". True though this may be, if a company cannot make money, jobs are removed, lives affected, and careers abruptly ended. Do the right thing because it's the right thing. Don't not do the right thing because leadership didn't include profitability when analyzing the other 50 things that might impact human behavior as a result of the most recent compensation plan.

Last (but not least) of these rings is that of the customer. I am amazed at how often people and companies treat their customers as though they are a nuisance. Make no mistake: Your company is a simple pass-through of services rendered by you to the customer. Your company takes a small cut of the action, but you are truly paid by the customer. You need to treat them as such every day.

I am not employing that exhausted "The customer is always right" mantra. I don't believe that to be true. I do believe the customer is, well, the customer, and deserves a certain level of appreciation, even respect. Two parties might have a heated interaction, voice competing perspectives and opinions, yet still reach an understanding. It happens in marriages every day (some with better results than others).

As in marriage, if you are inflexible and contentious, disrespectful and rude, dismissive of the other person's needs and wants, and dishonest in your everyday dealings with them, I assure you that divorce lies ahead. Your customer is no different. So, build a team and organization that rewards and encourages employees for adhering to these core human qualities.

Leadership & Its Meaning

New and young leaders often struggle to understand leadership in practical terms. Because the word is synonymous with such gray terminology as "management," "micromanagement," and "boss," its more fundamental properties are often rendered opaque.

Admittedly, plenty of leaders within the sales arena do exhibit managerial and boss-like tendencies. This is often a by-product of inherent personality characteristics. In other instances, it speaks to what a given team, department, or office might require in order to function well. But I maintain that managers and bosses do not yield results on par with those of genuine leaders.

A checkbook can be managed, as can a calendar. People, I contend, are not checkbooks or calendars. They cannot be managed in so simple a manner. What they can be, however, is empowered, held to account, provided with structure, and challenged to achieve success beyond what they once imagined was possible.

Try doing any of these for a checkbook.

To manage a person is to assume dictatorial control of their schedule and of their daily tasks.

"Report at X hour."

"Eat lunch at Y hour."

"Don't leave prior to Z hour."

If this is your approach to leadership, allow me to offer my congratulations—you have made yourself replaceable by an Outlook calendar. Well done.

A former employee of mine called to jokingly explain that he "...had been working way too hard." I took the bait and asked him to explain. Apparently, his boss (notice my word choice there) had sent a team-wide e-mail to call out a few people for leaving the office at too early a time; that being 5:30, as I understood it. My former employee, always a top performer and almost always in the office until 6:30 or 7:00, was demoralized by the email.

Why?

Because he had been working late of his own accord, not because he felt obligated to do so. His motivations were his own.

A true leader will master the art of motivating people to achieve a common goal. And it *is* an art, certainly more so than it is a science.

Of singular importance to achieving a sense of shared purpose is making certain that everyone understands that purpose in the first place. If not, your efforts will amount to an exercise in futility. I find myself regularly amazed by the gray zone many leaders operate in, as they assume their people are perfectly clear on the team's success metrics. When meeting with those teams, I often come away with a unique success metric explanation for every single rep I speak with.

Fixing this is easy.

Take the time to generate an expectations document outlining monthly, quarterly, or annual quotas, along with dialing minimums, appointment requirements, added contact goals, new deal prospects, et cetera. Do this with the mindset of a leader, not a manager. In other words, keep the requirements manageable and allow for latitude should a given rep prove successful in following their own path.

Remember: A company thrives on revenue, not dial reports. Get the cash in the door, worry about the dials and close ratios only as a means to an end.

My belief is that the right team will recognize expectations as they are provided and problems as they arise. Allow for their own intelligence to find its footing in achieving the collective goal.

A Few Stray Observations

The author Aldous Huxley once wrote, "Most human beings have an almost infinite capacity for taking things for granted."

That statement is as true in business as anywhere else in life, maybe more so. I spoke in chapter one about how making assumptions has led to many mistakes in my career. A manager takes for granted that his people know the company values, know the company's core services, know the correct pricing, know the correct Terms & Conditions, know the cancellation policy, know their own quota.

A leader takes *none* of these things for granted.

At least not at first.

Eventually, once the team is fine-tuned and operating with a strong understanding as to how their goals might best be realized, a leader can get out of the way and watch their preparation and training bear fruit.

Stray Observation # 1

Not every sales professional needs a ton of guidance to meet or exceed their quota. Provide them with the ideal end result and they will forge ahead, roadmap be damned. While most of your reps will imagine themselves to be of this caliber, most are in fact not. They can surely hit individual targets, but these must be identified for them by a sensible and competent leader.

A study some years past revealed that 80% of licensed drivers feel they are better than average when it comes to skillfully operating a motor vehicle. Do the math on that one and get back to me with your findings.

Individual contributors and leaders are no different. While a few take flight on their own with little to no direction, these are the exceptions. They are not the norm. The majority of people need a fairly detailed road map of success to get from point A to point Z. Your job as a leader is to give it to them. All of them.

Again, on assumptions, don't assume that someone is one of the rare beings that can fly on their own. That designation is something that must be earned with results. That person cannot just tell you. They must show you, and until you see the results, they get treated the same as everyone else.

Stray Observation #2

Your reps are now your clients. Sure, you may not be selling anymore, but your people are your accounts—treat them as such. Consider the effort you put forth when creating those sales wins that ultimately yielded your promotion to a leadership position. Now transfer that same time, effort, and creativity to the work of leading your individual contributors to sales success of their own.

Let's say you have just been promoted from an individual contributor position. In that job, your quota was $800,000 per year. You hit that quota by selling into four or five accounts per year. Now you are managing a team of ten people with the same quota. You cannot win by selling 40 to 50 accounts. You will win by treating these ten people like your accounts. You will understand their individual strengths and weaknesses. You will uncover areas where they need additional development, and you will learn where you need to sell them on concepts that are critical to their success. Your job is to develop them into successful producers. It's about them. Not you! As Harry Truman once noted, "It is amazing what you can accomplish if you do not care who gets the credit."

Divorce yourself from the credit equation entirely. You've had your day in the sun; now let others shine as you once did.

Stray Observation #3

Turnover can be pricey. Strike that—turnover is *almost always* pricey. A new-hire breakeven point for some sales organizations can be a year or more in the realizing. Bear that in mind and take regular inventory of your company's largest deals/accounts. The reasoning is simple: Customer turnover is often tied directly to rep turnover. View reps with large book sizes as customers first, employees second.

Which is not to say you allow them to run roughshod over you, over their colleagues, or over the company; it is instead to say that you do all you can to ensure their value to the company is adequately conveyed. It also means you find ways to maximize their subsequent sales efforts.

Lightning often strikes twice.

~~~

We're now warmed up. Let's continue this conversation in the chapters ahead.

Chapter III:
Why Were You Chosen to Lead?

I ONCE TOOK OVER AN OFFICE that was in terrible form. The office was an inside sales division that housed a sales director, multiple sales leaders, and around 50 inside sales reps. When I first arrived on scene, I was doing a lot of my due diligence. Digging into team performance, trying to understand the processes that were in place, inquiring about who the best and worst performers on the team were, and trying to get a feel for where the key gaps were and why they were there.

After I had all the answers, I pulled the leadership team together. I asked a simple (but loaded) question. "Can you explain to me your process for creating success?" After a bit of an awkward silence, someone finally spoke up. "We (the leadership team) like to walk around the floor and talk trash to the reps.". I thought the others would somehow squash this explanation or come up with something better, but they didn't. They all nodded in agreement. They even went on in more detail. "Yeah, we sort of walk around and challenge one another. People really like it.". Really? Now I have heard some pretty bad answers to this question over the years, but this one is the grand prize winner. I would have preferred to hear that they had no strategy. The mere thought that this was a perceived strategy or process blew my mind. That is not a plan, a strategy, or even rational. This team had been in a rapid decline for at least a year and a half. Talking trash was not working!

We quickly made changes to the leadership team. We implemented process and accountability. It did not take long to turn this business around. In fact, it went from the worst in the company to the best in six months.

Bottom line: you need a strategy and a process to find success.

Why were you chosen for leadership?

Whenever I ask someone to describe their leadership responsibilities, I hear many answers...most of them what you would expect: "Grow my revenue," "Grow the business," "Gain greater market share," "Kick our #1 competitor's ass," and so on. They are largely good answers and they align with every standard expectation, but they do not in and of themselves address the question of why *you* were promoted.

You were chosen for the role because the company wants you to replicate yourself, or at least share your qualities with others destined for leadership. The only way to achieve this is to teach people both what you do and how you do it. And the only way to teach people to do what you do is to cultivate a process, teach that process, and hold your protégés accountable to following that process. Period.

Take the NFL. Every team has a head coach, and every head coach runs their team a little differently than every other head coach. Bill Belichick, head coach of the New England Patriots, runs his team very differently than Pete Carroll in Seattle. Both coaches (as of this writing) are very successful, but if you left the Seattle Seahawks and Pete Carroll for the New England Patriots, you would certainly not be playing the game the same way. This is because each coach cultivates a system into which talent is meant to fit, to play a specific role. Coaches condition and train their talent to understand these systems, then hold the players accountable to performing well within them.

Business leadership is no different (the absence of tackles aside). Once you craft a workable system, your responsibility is to plug in good people, teach them the process, develop them, and make accountability the bedrock of your professional framework. In following this simple process, adding newcomers to the system is surprisingly easy. Once up and running, it is quite literally a plug-and-play process.

Before you can go through the process of shaping your personal keys to success, you must first define your personal formula for success. There will be different answers for literally each person. It is important that you devote close thought to the things that have made you successful every day. Second, what do you do that allows you to be the best at this special thing?. And third, if you were going to teach someone to do this thing, how would you teach them and how would you go about inspecting to ensure that the thing was being done?

Let's break this down further, starting with the success factor, which can literally be anything that you do/did that lead to your success. There are usually multiples of these, and they are not always as evident as you might think. We tend to accumulate small techniques over thousands of interactions and through a series of executions. Over time we internalize them, subconsciously, into our daily routine. You may know you are good. You inherently do these "things" that make you stand out. These are the things you need to be able to consciously acknowledge.

Inevitably, you are successful due to multiple contributing factors. In sales, it may be things like knowledge of the customer's business. Other things include, but are not limited to: building strong customer relationships, possessing strong negotiation skills, and excelling at deal qualification. Regardless of your unique attributes, the first step to creating the replicable process is to acknowledge and understand those attributes.

Once you figure out *what* you do, the next step is to figure out *how* you do it. What are the techniques you employed to achieve this result? This part seems to come a little easier once the success factor is acknowledged. Most of us, however, tend to believe that everyone does these things already, or that they at least know to do them. This is clearly not the case. If it were true, you would not stand out. You would not be in leadership.

But you *are.*

Now that you know what made you a success, and how you realized as much, you need to create a process to support it. This process will be the cornerstone of your team's success, so it is critical that you put considerable thought into it. Later in the chapter, I will walk you through my approach to problem solving. This is very much the same kind of process. Here you want to create systems that literally force people to perform a series of steps, which ultimately yield an identical success factor, regardless of the given scenario.

Forcing people to learn is critical. You will want to teach by example. Next, you will give them an exercise, one in which they follow your example through to completion. And, last, they will present to you their completed work. Once they do so, you will give them feedback, then have them redo the exercise if necessary (perhaps multiple times) until it is where you believe it needs to be.

Finally, and most important of all, there is the matter of inspection. Here you are ensuring the success factor has become "sticky". I always recommend completing the first exercise, training them on the process, and executing on the learning exercise. Once you have this complete, you will want scale. What I mean here is that the initial example has been done. Now you want to have a rollout plan. For example, five accounts by next week completed, fifteen accounts by the end of the month, and so on.

So, let's perform a practical exercise. Take 10 to 15 minutes and write down each of the things you did as an individual contributor to achieve success. Leave nothing out.

1)_____

_____

2)_____

_____

3)_____

_____

4)_____

_____

5)_____

_____

6)_____

_____

7)_____

_____

There is no right or wrong answer. There is only your answer.

Okay, you have made your list; now how do we create the system? Let's use a few of the following examples:

1.) I know my customer better than they know themselves

So how do you do this today? Maybe you always know some key things about your customer. Perhaps there are ways you drill down into accounts. Perhaps it's surveys, et cetera.

What process could you implement to ensure your people are as versed in their customers as you were in yours?

Here are a few thoughts:

➢ Create a research template (Excel, SF, MSDynamics) encompassing the fields you typically prioritize when blueprinting or researching accounts. This might include things like: 1. company size, 2. locations, 3. fiscal cycle, 4. budget, 5. how they make money, 6. top three challenges, 7. three ways your product could impact each challenge, 8. organizational charts, et cetera.

➢ Once completed, fill out the sheet in its entirety (using an actual account) and show your people how you gathered all of the data, where you found it, and the tricks you employed to back into more elusive information.

➢ Next, ask each rep to complete two of these templates prior to their next meeting and have each person present their findings to the team, along with what they learned and how they plan on using the information.

➢ Continue this process until your team's top opportunities have undergone the same level of scrutiny. People will likely see the value and continue on their own, but holding them accountable to completing the exercise is also recommended. Giving them a set number of accounts to complete and a date by which to complete the exercise will help in pulling this through.

➢ Lastly, inspect them. Make sure to review them for completeness and for mistakes. Give them feedback on ways to better think through them, or to find answers.

Another common example of a successful sales practice is the following:

2.)   I always met with multiple buyers in an account

Are there systematic steps you could implement in order to encourage meeting with multiple buyers?

➢ Conduct a training centered on how best to identify new buyers/locations within one of your team's accounts. One way to do this would be to identify the buyers in your own company if you were selling your product or service to yourself. Undoubtedly this would demonstrate the depths you could go to in other companies, if you simply knew them as well as you know your own organization.

➢ Implement a weekly accountability measure focused on meeting with *new contacts*, as opposed to meetings with familiar clients.

➢ Prospect on a Friday with the specific aim of acquiring contacts in, say, Chicago when their account is based in, say, Dallas. Encourage them to explore beyond corporate headquarters.

> ➤ Book travel to a given city. Anyone with at least three scheduled appointments is invited to join you.

I used sales examples here, but these are easily converted into any functional area. You have done exceptional things to get to where you are today, so all you must do is think about your areas of strength and build out a similar framework.

There is no shortage of possibilities where achieving this goal is concerned. The key is that you cannot simply tell your people what to do; you must teach them, hold them accountable, and subject their efforts to strict scrutiny. Again, the goal is self-replication!

Now that you have an idea, look at your list of successful behaviors and write down the answers to the following questions for EACH of the items you listed above:

1) Why are they not doing this today?
   a. lack of skill/knowledge,
   b. a lack of ability, or
   c. a lack of belief.

You must pick which one. If it is lack of skill or knowledge, you must teach; if lack of belief, you must sell them; if lack of ability, you must replace them. These are all easier said than done, but no honest soul has ever characterized leadership as being an easy path; certainly not me. But leadership tends to pick the person, not the other way around. If you are possessed of those qualities which make a good leader, your professional circumstances will almost certainly steer you toward management, oversight, or a command of some sort. This is as true of the business arena as it is of any human collective, be it the military, the manufacturing industry, or professional sports. Not every excellent contributor possesses the mental fortitude or deep understanding of interpersonal dynamics to be a good coach. Likewise, not every first-rate sales representative can export their talent and knowledge for the good of a sales team.

But if you are able to do those things, you will likely find yourself promoted accordingly. Which will mean frequently making hard choices or performing challenging tasks.

Teaching a skill requires knowledge not only of the skill itself, but also of how people learn and what steps are necessary to ensure a lesson is retained. Depending on the skills you need to instill or the mindset you need to encourage, your methods might involve routine role-playing sessions, company blueprinting exercises, or mock account reviews. Retention is key, which means repetition will almost certainly prove necessary. Gauge each protégé and make certain to correctly assess their level of engagement with your teachings. And remember to back off when appropriate; it's easy to overreach when attempting to shoehorn a lot of information into a condensed training module.

Selling someone on why it is they should believe as you believe (essentially evangelizing) is particularly tough within a sales organization. Ever tried to sell a sales person? It's certainly achievable, but their mental barriers are reliably more difficult to overcome. Once again, if you weren't capable in the first place, you wouldn't be called upon for a task of that sort...and you wouldn't be reading this book. But you *are* reading this book, which suggests you *are* capable of selling a person on the importance of an activity, which means you must condition yourself for the work of doing so when necessary and provision your psychological toolkit with the mechanisms necessary for a successful outcome.

As for replacing people—it is never fun. Nobody likes doing it, and with good reason. You risk seriously undermining the self-image and confidence of the person being let go, to say nothing of imperiling their financial wellbeing. But it is often the only sensible recourse if a given role simply isn't a good fit...for the company or for them. After all, you aren't doing a person any favors by allowing them to persist in an occupation or an organization with which their skills and capabilities do not properly align. If your instincts tell you to phase the person out while they find employment elsewhere, do as you see fit. But do not allow the situation to fester. The result will be harmful for all involved.

2)   What will you do to correct it?

a. Lack of skill/knowledge – what sort developmental training can you create to teach them? With sales being an inherently interpersonal profession (one of the last, it seems), interactive trainings are advisable, perhaps even essential. I've elaborated on this below, but bear in mind the value of evaluating your reps under realistic training circumstances. And invest in dependable recording technology. Objective scrutiny is best achieved when we see ourselves as others see us. This point will become clearer as you read on.

b. Lack of belief – what information will you share to sell them? Selling is a psychologically taxing phenomenon. In attempting a sale, you are essentially engaging in a mental contest of sorts, laboring aggressively to have your way of thinking properly understood by the other party. In the sales profession, we build up a thick skin to withstand the repeated assault of outright rejection. We try to remind ourselves of the trenches when we eventually make it to the clouds, but it's all too easy to forget.

A surefire way to remember that feeling is to engage in the often-thankless work of selling a fellow sales person, as alluded to above. The fact is, no matter how talented or well-trained your sales team might be, absent a strong belief in the product/service they are selling, their effort will invariably suffer. They must be instilled with a sense of purpose, with a sense of connection to the idea they are ultimately being asked to broadcast.

Product belief or belief in an idea is not just relevant to sales. Regardless of the functional area you run, it is important that you foster belief in your methodology. The way to do that is through data and success stories.

The best thing you can offer upon finding that belief has diminished within your ranks is context and broader understanding. Context in terms of how your widget ties in to a clear need of some sort, and understanding as to where your organization fits into the larger industry landscape. When neither context nor understanding is present, your sales professionals are prone to behaving as though they exist in a corporate vacuum, one capable of sucking up belief and diminishing effort at once. Educate yourself aggressively and instill knowledge frequently. In doing so, you will safeguard your team's collective belief from the ever-present threat of apathy.

Motivation is an elusive commodity in the modern corporate arena, particularly with sales pros eagerly shopping new opportunities on a routine basis. I am firmly of the mind that creating a sense of connection between your reps and your company's mission statement will yield you tremendous dividends in terms of professional loyalty and strong sales. That's the very definition of a win-win scenario; but it must be earned—you must learn to sell salespeople. That's no mean feat.

c. Lack of ability - what sort of people or skill-sets are necessary to achieve success? Identifying the right sort of person/skill-set for your sales team is as much a matter of evaluating what a poor fit is lacking as what the right fit possesses. Take for example a situation where you've hired someone based in large part on their excellent personal bearing and perfunctory resumé bullet points (B.A. in Business, finance courses, et cetera). This person appears (on the surface) to be a solid hire; at a minimum, they can be counted upon to not embarrass the company when meeting with clients. Well-spoken, courteous, some sense of business lingo, and so on.

But a month or so in, it becomes apparent that your hire with the excellent personal bearing and the perfunctory resumé bullet points is simply not a dynamic thinker. Maybe they belong in the perfectly respectable and necessary fields of life insurance or financial advising. These require their own unique talents and training and might suit your hire well. The reality, however, is that,in this example, you are not working in those fields. You happen to sell a service which functions more abstractly and requires an agile mind to effectively understand and subsequently articulate.

When it comes time to replace this otherwise solid employee, you must take inventory of what specifically was absent within their skill-set. The negative space they've been occupying will bring your desired attributes into sharper relief. No matter your industry, this principle applies. Not every motorcycle sales professional could sell software or any such intangible item, agreed? Okay, so reflect on these ideas closely and come away from this chapter with a stronger sense of your most ideal candidate. There will be compromises along the way (there always are), but interviewing potential sales professionals after having carefully considered what you truly need will reduce the likelihood of your making a bad hire.

3) How will you see the exercise through to fruition? This is where 95% of people fail. Often, the best trainers are the worst teachers. They provide great, elaborate trainings only to have people partially engage with the information, if at all. You must create a process by which people hear you, perform the task(s) for themselves, then demonstrate clear competency thereof. This may require several attempts before success is realized. An example of this worth sharing is a training I designed and carried out some years ago. The training centered on helping my salespeople to conduct *relevant* sales meetings. Any sales manager worth their salt knows what I mean by "relevant" in this context. It is the difference between daylight hours being spent strategically and being misspent cripplingly. Most of my people were relying on 30-page PowerPoint presentations (a sales tool I generally disapprove of) when running their meetings, which resulted in their listing out all our products and associated sales pitches and spins. They were blasting through their "discussions" without once stopping to ask a question of the client, nor seeking to qualify whether the material being presented was in any way relevant. To help fix this, I allowed each sales rep to choose one account for an exercise in which they would present a sales pitch to the team. There were some key rules:

    a. You cannot have a slide in the presentation if it does not address a *specific* client issue or need

    b. You must be able to articulate and "connect the dots" of each presented product to a specific and tangibly identifiable problem

    c. You must be able to achieve a conversational tone/style within the sales pitch (the difference between speaking *with* someone and speaking *to* someone).

I conducted the first of these, then gave everyone a week to replicate my approach. We recorded each person as well to allow them the benefit of viewing themselves as others see them. We gathered at 7:30 each morning to conduct these role-playing exercises.

I required that each observer write down **at least two suggestions** for each presenter which, if acted upon, could improve the overall presentation quality. The primary reason for this was to prevent the exercise from descending into a festival of mindlessly encouraging praise and mutual adulation. The input needed to be objective and constructive, or else we had effectively wasted everyone's time.

Anyway, we began a week later, as planned; nobody nailed it on the first try. A couple of people didn't get it until the fourth. I then followed through (an essential aspect of leadership) by undertaking a schedule of observing each rep on multiple appointments, taking notes during the meeting, and sharing the feedback via a post-sales meeting sheet. Results were as follows: 1. the team dramatically improved in this critical skill, and 2. the following quarter saw us enjoying measurably increased sales and revenue. The investment of time yielded a return in dollars. Every now and again, rolling up your sleeves is necessary to keep your sales trajectory moving up and to the right.

This is an example of identifying a key area for improvement, creating a process, and forcing people to learn and, more importantly, to internalize a specific skill. Measures of this sort require a great deal of patience on the part of the leader. Believe me, keeping your team motivated during a 7:30 training is not an easy task, not even for a naturally enthusiastic person. You will need to summon up ample energy of your own to maintain a feeling of momentum and purpose. Fortunately, energy is contagious; wield it generously.

4) To what specifically will you hold your people accountable? Will it be a daily, weekly, monthly, or quarterly metric? And what *is* the metric? Why, in your opinion, is *that* metric the right one?

5) How will you hold your people accountable? In life, all activities are coupled with consequence. Consequences are often regarded as invariably negative, but there are always counter, or positive, consequences to negative ones. If you eat poorly and abstain from exercise, your health will inevitably suffer. The reverse is also true: eat well and exert yourself physically, and your image and vitality will reflect as much. You must decide what the negative *and* positive consequences are for achieving or not achieving a given goal. Publish this in writing for your people and ensure that they recognize the accountability implied therein.

6) What will you measure? And how often? A process devoid of data collection is a process destined to fail. If the process works, this is great data

to share with your team. If it is not working, you may need to reformulate its mechanics. This will also help you identify new areas of focus or development within the team dynamic.

As mentioned before, most leaders fail in the pull-through aspect of this approach. They are perfectly capable of grasping the "personal formula for success" concept and can create pertinent trainings and tools for the benefit of their people. But where they fail is in holding people accountable; arguably the most crucial element.

Training is not merely a checklist, nor is it is a matter of *what* you teach. It is entirely about <u>what your people retain</u>. You might be the most gifted teacher on earth, capable of engaging your mentees with dynamic lessons. But if your people depart the training having retained little to nothing, then you have failed.

Pull-through requires you develop a process that will literally *force* people into embracing, inhabiting, and embodying your formula; thus, our having previously written out the process information. The key is to ensure that you make no assumptions about your people, especially about their ability to perform well in the status quo. Promotions into leadership roles are often the result of a predecessor having failed to perform adequately. For that reason, you need to act quickly in implementing your system with respect to moving people in the right direction.

Conversely, if you find yourself taking over for a well-performing leader who was likewise promoted, I highly recommend you nevertheless implement your own system. Very rarely will you find the "If it's not broken, don't fix it" maxim to be applicable when assuming a leadership role. The reason is that individuals operate and view the world distinctively from one another. Having been a leader of leaders, I have never replaced a leader due to promotion or demotion without the newly appointed individual expressing to me how "messed up" they found things to be. Though not necessarily true in every instance, people do place value on different things and prioritize their efforts based on their unique strengths and capabilities. They also tend to become trapped in ways of thinking, based on beliefs in their abilities or perceived inabilities. Let's look at that more closely.

Belief is an interesting thing.

When I talk about "selling" people to realize progress, it seems like an accessible concept. The truth is that identifying and overcoming an individual's psychological barriers to success is hugely complex work. These barriers can be easily overcome, in some cases; but make no mistake—many such barriers can be difficult to both recognize and surmount.

Which brings me to Englishman Roger Bannister...and to the four-minute mile.

Roger's overcoming of a major psychological barrier is a favorite story of mine. It speaks both to human potential and to overcoming self-imposed limitations.

By the mid-20th century, no runner in recorded history had ever completed a mile in under four minutes' time. It was therefore regarded as being impossible. The thinking went like this: "Because it *hasn't* been done, it *cannot* be done." Now talk about a self-defeating mentality.

Roger Bannister was not convinced. And on May 6, 1954, the former Olympian (and future neurologist) achieved what "knowledgeable" authorities had said could not be done: Bannister ran a mile in under four minutes. His exact time was 3:59.4, a record which stood for around six weeks. Which meant not only had Bannister shattered a barrier, he had opened the door for others to do the same.

The weather was questionable, the science/knowledge underpinning his efforts was shaky, and the track was rough by modern standards—Bannister overcame all of this to achieve the impossible.

Further demonstrating the importance of belief, Bannister himself was quoted as saying, "I knew enough medicine and physiology to know it wasn't a physical barrier, but I think it had become a psychological barrier."

This was proven to be far more than Bannister's opinion when, astonishingly, his record was beaten 46 days later by Swedish runner John Landy. It was a difference of 1.5 seconds, which given what was deemed possible 46 days earlier, may as well have been 1.5 hours. The following year, 10 runners accomplished the same feat. Since then, more than 500 Americans alone have achieved this feat. It is now the standard by which competitive milers are judged.

I shared this story during a leadership training years ago to highlight that instilling in people a belief in their ability to achieve a goal can yield profound results. At the time, our company held only two accounts over the $1M revenue mark (maybe three). Our closest competitor had over 70, despite ours being a superior product. Not to mention, our customer relationships were stronger, and we certainly had better sales people. The issue, it seemed, was that our people either did not see or did not believe in their ability to acquire deal sizes of that caliber. They were impeded not by the reality of the situation, but by self-imposed limitations.

In addressing this, we set out on a mission to demonstrate the true opportunity within each rep's book of business. We assembled the senior leadership team for a full week and went through literally *every* account in the Fortune 500. For each account, we reviewed things such as company size, company revenues, employee turnover, industry, hires per year, and a variety of secondary/tertiary factors.

Once I had organized our findings, we actively debated as to what we could truly offer each company in the way of services. We also placed a reasonable value on each account. Because everyone was involved in creating the new target values for the companies, the leaders were also equipped to explain to the sales people why the value was set to the amount that it was, and how we reached that conclusion.

Our final step was to build a compensation plan around the new expectation. We gave each rep five target accounts with pre-determined values. Bonuses were paid to them based on achieving the prescribed target within the specific account. In effect, if Company A had a target of $1M, the only way to earn the target bonus was to reach $1M in that account. If they sold company B for $1M, it did not count. Essentially, each rep had to hit one target account of the five assigned to make their number.

And if they hit all five...it was a nice year for them.

There was, at first, a lot of pushback from the sales team. Everyone thought we were crazy. "There is no way we will ever be able to secure those deal values," they moaned. We went to work anyway.

By the end of the first year, we had secured 26 $1M+ deals. By the end of the second year, we exceeded our competitor in this regard. The $1M+ became less of a rarity. It was not the norm, but nor was it an anomaly either. We did not spend time training them on how to position the product differently. We did not train them on anything new that year. We only talked about how much these accounts were worth and how much money they were going to make when they hit those target bonuses. Belief was the key.

Give the power of belief its due.

With all that in mind, let's review what we've covered so far.

Make sure to clearly articulate those practices which contributed to your own success. Leave nothing out. Next, develop a process by which to ensure your people effectively pull-through in emulating those clearly articulated practices.

Hold each team member accountable to routinely measure the plan's effectiveness. We will explore this to a far greater extent in subsequent chapters. Lastly, instill a sense of belief in your people wherever possible. The dividends could be enormous.

Now, on to accountability.

Accountability:

Accountability is hands down among my favorite concepts as it pertains to effective leadership. It is also the most likely pitfall to entrap and ultimately break new leaders. The word "accountability" has, by its very nature, a negative connotation; I hope to sell you on why it should not be regarded as such.

Human psychology on this matter is profoundly interesting. From early childhood, we crave structure and accountability, but also cannot resist the instinct to test its limits. If you have children, you are closely aware of this phenomenon. You have likely witnessed the three-year-old child whose parents plead, "Johnny, don't do that. Johnny, I said stop. One...two...three... Johnny, don't make me get up. Johnny, if you do that one more time, I'm going to put you in timeout.". It is exactly as painful to channel via the written word as it is to witness firsthand. That child knows his behavior is effectively coupled with no real consequences; with no (you guessed it) accountability. The child acts out, is unpleasant to be around, and is generally unsuccessful at assimilating into the general playground population. It's a loss all around.

I can remember countless 'Super Nanny' episodes in which the eponymous Super Nanny would enter a house with a child who resembled Satan himself. The scenario played out identically from one episode to the next:

- ➢ Child exhibits miserable behavior
- ➢ Parents are overwhelmed, frustrated, at the end of their rope
- ➢ Parents can't understand why their little angel acts so differently from all the other kids.
- ➢ Nanny identifies 1. lack of structure, and 2. accountability
- ➢ Nanny implements structure and accountability measures
- ➢ Child resists for a time
- ➢ Child's instincts and needs take hold
- ➢ Child transforms from Satan to saint
- ➢ Wave magic wand—Presto!

Fast-forward twenty-five years and we find the human brain, at its most basic level, is not so different. Although we verbally reject the need for structure and accountability, we realize we do in fact need (and want) both.

So, given that accountability is a critical leadership ingredient, why do so many leaders struggle with the concept? Answer: The vast majority of leaders enter a role with a few too many assumptions in hand. The first assumption is that everyone will do what needs to be done simply because they are good people. As mentioned earlier, I do believe everyone *wants* to do well. But I don't believe that everyone knows *how* to do well.

Accountability reliably bridges that divide.

The second assumption leaders make is that metrics and accountability measures will be met with reflexive resistance. In my experience, leaders are disliked for one reason: They failed to make their people successful. If your aim is to be liked, you must teach your people how to win. They may not always like the process, but they will respect you as a leader for showing them the way. At the end of the day, I care far more about gaining someone's respect than I do about our afterhours socializing, or lack thereof. Leadership is a long, selfless, and tiresome journey; and your goal, I imagine, is to continue climbing the leadership ladder. The only way that happens is to achieve results. I will forever champion the idea that accountability is essential to this pursuit.

Now, let's examine the components of accountability.

What to Measure

First, we must determine what it is we will be measuring. A former leader of mine often argued that "activity is always the problem, never the answer." Meaning that, when things were not going well, people always went back to the basics of dials/appointments. These are merely the remedial components of success. Understanding the problem requires looking beyond those items to identify the root cause. Rarely is the problem a matter of meetings, a lack of viable buyers, or insufficient deal proposals. When deciding what metrics to track, we want to make sure we are driving activities and behaviors that lead to success. Which is, of course, easier said than done.

The goal is to first decide what you need to focus on. In our earlier exercise, you identified several factors which will prove essential to your leadership formula. Now it is important to identify areas of opportunity within the business. This is in addition to teaching people to replicate your success formula.

One word of caution here: Make certain you don't do too much at one time. I like to proceed with three to four things (on the high end) per year as primary focal items. Any more than this, and it becomes difficult to effectively pull-through.

With so many things to choose from, where do you start? Below is a list of commonly tracked sales-specific activities/functions:

Talk time
Dials
Appointments Set
Appointments Completed
Appointment Conversion Rate
Appointment-to-Close Ratio
Proposals
Pipeline
Pipeline Conversion %
Time-to-Close
Specific Product sales
Discount %
YTD/MTD % to Plan
Dollars Closed
New Dollars Closed
Renewal Rate
Renewal Upsell Amount

Depending on the level of sales on which your team operates, dials, talk time, and appointments may be an important metric for your organization. This has been dissected many ways by many companies, but is essentially a generic metric with no real substance. I contend that it *could* be meaningful if the necessary sub-filters are applied. For example, a given company strongly encourages employees to identify and sell to multiple buyers within an organization. As a result, they measure unique dials and also appointments with new contacts. This yields the predictable result of encouraging reps to identify new buyers with the aim of satisfying these metrics. They are compelled to constantly blueprint and prospect for new buyers, which ultimately leads to their closing more business.

Proposals per month is another metric I would qualify as going beyond basic activity. It may seem simple enough, but I have observed many organizations allowing their sales force to import earlier proposals into current months, thus yielding stale pipelines and an absence of new proposals. If this were identified as an important metric, it would be critical to ensure that we measure new proposals each month, rather than the accumulation of proposals drawn from past months or quarters. If 200K in freshly proposed business is expected each month, I should literally have that in new proposals within a thirty-day timeframe, rather than 150K this month and 50K from the previous.

You need to spend time thinking through to the desired result. Your sales representatives should be closely aware of their respective quotas, as well as how the metrics serve as a formula for the achievement of those quotas.

At the same time, you must be careful to avoid evangelizing on the subject numbers for their own sake. Understand that adults (like children) are given to testing the limits of accountability. In many cases, the numbers can be easily changed, altered, and achieved without reshaping behavior. One example I would offer is a proposal-focus which I experienced firsthand. We generated a proposal quota for each salesperson. The result was exactly what we had asked for—a system rife with new proposals. The salespeople simply reduced each proposal into a series of subdivisions within the system. Presto! Each salesperson reached the number, but we did nothing to earn more sales revenue. We immediately addressed the problem, but also took inventory of the fact that we had received that for which we had asked. Ensure that the metrics you track ultimately lead to success. Otherwise, they are merely numbers on a spreadsheet or in a SalesForce report.

The interrelated subjects of accountability and metrics will appear frequently throughout the coming chapters.

Chapter IV:
Holding Others (and Oneself) Accountable

TWO REPUTATIONS HAVE FOLLOWED ME around during my time in leadership. One is that I am a jerk. The second is that I am unquestionably one of the most consistent performers relative to my peers.

Period.

The latter reputation was propagated by my bosses and by the CEO. The former by those outside of my sphere of influence and who otherwise did not know me personally.. It was largely held that I am tough, but fair. I am referred to by some as the "Candor Monster," by others as "Grandpa," and others almost certainly employed monikers which don't warrant printing.

But, mostly, I am just known as Will. The somewhat reclusive, slightly scary guy who most could never get a read on.

This is due to my largely introverted nature. Yes, I realize that quality is somewhat at odds with the typical characterization of a sales leader. I'm perfectly happy to buck that stereotype.

A quick side note about my entry into sales, which is a very different story in relation to most others in this business. As you will recall, growing up, all I wanted was to find a way to make a lot of money. One day, I rather randomly met a lady. She was driving a Cadillac, was dressed to the nines, she was very sharp. I asked her what she did for a living and she simply handed me her card. I don't remember her name or what company she worked for, but the title on her card simply read "Sales.". That's when I decided mine would be a career in sales. I didn't even know what "Sales" meant, at least not in its broader context. In my mind, the only sales I knew about were car related, but she certainly did not work for a dealership.

I wanted what she had.

I was a very introverted kid. I did not have many friends growing up, and the thought of engaging in random conversations with complete strangers scared me a bit. So, I told myself that day (the same day I got that card) that I was going to introduce myself to someone new every day for the next month and start some sort of conversation. I made good on that promise to myself, but to this day, it is still not easy for me...though I *am* good at it.

Anyway, back to my being a jerk...

In the early years of my leadership career, I was very blunt. And as I stated in the opening chapter, there is an important distinction between being blunt and being candid. Being blunt makes you a jerk; being candid makes you an effective leader. As a less mature leader, I didn't care if I made someone cry, could care less if I hurt someone's feelings. The message was the message and I put little thought into my delivery. In my mind, if someone was screwing up, they needed to know about it...immediately.

I still believe in giving quick and immediate feedback, but I approach it differently now. Most leaders (most *people*) tend to shy away from confrontation and from tough conversations. They imagine that ignoring a problem will result in its going away, or assume the person causing the problem is aware of the issue, therefore negating the need to add insult to injury.

This mentality may be sustainable in a non-sales environment, though I suggest you not take that possibility for granted. Within a sales environment, it is crippling. And I can assert that with absolute certainty. Knowing when and how to address a problem is essential for any leader. The "when" we have already discussed: immediately, and quickly. As for the how, well, read on.

Mastering the art of communication is critical in any leadership role. A sales team, office, or organization of any size is ultimately governed to one degree or another by the leader or leadership groups charged with growing revenue. In what universe could a team, office, or organization enact the strategies or pitching approaches envisioned by their leaders, if those leaders have not communicated such things in any coherent, accessible manner?

The realization of any plan involving more than a single person must be paired with communication equal to the task of conveying its most essential aspects. If your plan entails nothing further than ensuring your sales rep meets you at the terminal by 9:00 A.M., your communication may be similarly simple.

"Hey, Mike."

"Yeah, Will?"

"Make sure you're at the gate by 9:00 tomorrow morning. I'd like to go over a few things before we reach Omaha."

"You got it."

The plan was simple, its execution intuitive, and its demands on both parties negligible. Your communication was achieved in a handful of syllables.

Now let's grow the complexity by several orders of magnitude. Imagine your office needs to exceed the previous quarter's revenue by at least 12% in order to achieve the company's goal. And let's say you are also being asked to expand sales of a certain product or service. It may well be that in fulfilling the latter, the former will also be covered. Or maybe not. But whatever you end up concluding in that regard, your office's sales teams need direction. Not every rep will necessarily see the larger picture; not every rep will even *care* to see the larger picture. But in crafting key goals around activity, products pitched, meetings set, et cetera, the achievement of your goal(s) is certainly within reach...*if you properly communicate the goals along with the steps necessary to place them within reach.*

Back to the subject of confrontation.

Another reason people tend to avoid confrontation, communication, et cetera is that, put plainly, people desire to be liked. This is directly attributable to the fact that ours is a remarkably social species. Our early survival depended on as much, as does our continued dominion over the planet. Individually, we don't fare very well in the wild. In groups, we thrive. But groups tend to order themselves via hierarchies, factions, families, classes, and so on. Within these sub-groups, individuals adopt different strategies to secure their place on the ladder. A strong but not overly articulate member might be respected but will find it difficult to garner feelings of affection from others in the group. Conversely, a charismatic individual might be able to get by with few actual skills, provided their pleasant and disarming presence can yield them a meal here and there.

Being liked carries with it different connotations than being respected. There are plenty of leaders I know well, but for whom I would never work. The list of people for whom I *would* work, go to battle with, and legitimately <u>respect</u> is a very short list. I want to work both with and for people I respect.

Respect is earned by one's actions, by winning, by effectively passing along their success formula. You like a leader or employee well enough to enjoy having drinks with them, but if they don't contribute to your overarching professional goals, over time you will grow to resent them. They will prove an impediment to your success and, by extension, ultimately cost you money.

Strive to be respected first; to be liked second.

In his book *Winning,* Jack Welch writes at some length on the subject of candor. He argues convincingly that in providing people with feedback, the good ones will self-correct. I adhere closely to this principle and have been pleased with the results. My people, good and bad, always knew where they stood in relation to their performance; how they ranked among their peers, and how close or distant they were from being out of the company.

My method of achieving as much includes both verbal and written communication. Verbal is fine, and certainly a good starting point, but if you want to get someone's attention, *really* let them know you are serious, put it in writing. Don't hide behind the written communication. You must first communicate verbally, as this is often enough to realize your desired result. But, failing that, you must follow up with clearly composed written communication.

This feedback circle, as I tend to envision it, is the cornerstone of accountability within your teams. It is plainly indispensable. When a new hire or recent transfer came aboard, I would sit down and communicate upfront the expectations of the job. Productivity metrics such as dials, appointments set, appointments completed, blueprinting of accounts, funnel expectations, close-ratios...all of it. I would then ask them what specifically they wanted to achieve. Were they wanting to make as much money as possible? Were they wanting to make 100% of their quota (no more and no less) and have a great work/life balance? Were they interested in moving up in the company? Each walked a different path and harbored a different set of expectations. This knowledge was very important, as it told me how to lead them. I will talk more about that later.

In leading leaders, I have spent a lot of time teaching the art and science of moving people in and out of plans. One lesson that I have consistently driven home from one leadership role to the next is how to make this part of their process. Put simply, I instruct others on the benefit of creating rules covering a. when people go on plan, b. what types of plans to implement based on the circumstances, c. formulating the consequences for not winning when on plan, and d. ultimately how reps are either removed from the plan or removed from the company. While my instruction and general philosophy remained relatively constant over time, I did at one point make a subtle change to my own process.

As I taught (and ultimately sold leaders on) this aspect of leadership, I fought against a constant fear my junior leaders expressed about implementing this type of accountability. Again, they feared this type of accountability would contribute to feelings of negativity throughout the ranks or would have people wanting to quit (spoiler: it never did, and they never quit...at least not the good ones). Nevertheless, in addressing this fear, I amended that crucial step preceding the first of three plans.

My original process was as follows:

Three months of missing monthly quota = Stage One Plan

Failure to meet expectations on Stage One Plan = Stage Two Plan

Failure to meet expectations on Stage Two Plan = Final Plan

Failure to meet expectations on Final Plan = Termination

I added another step, which went as follows:

Two months of not hitting monthly quota = **Safety Net Plan**

Failure to show improvement from the Safety Net Plan (Soft Plan) = Stage One Plan

Failure to meet expectations on Stage One Plan = Stage Two Plan

Failure to meet expectations on Stage Two Plan = Final Plan

Failure to meet expectations on Final Plan = Termination

You're likely curious as to what I mean by Safety Net (Soft) Plan. Well, let's take a closer look.

The Safety Net/Soft Plan

The Safety Net (or Soft) Plan is an interim means of trying to save reps from finding themselves moved to a Hard Plan, or a Plan-Plan, as some term it. As in, *"You mean I'm on an actual Plan-Plan? You've gotta be kidding me."* The concept is simple: You and the rep are certainly having a performance discussion, but with one notable nuance—you add a talk-track along the lines of the following:

Soft Plan Talk-Track

"Mary, I wanted to have a discussion with you today to talk about your performance. You have missed your target for the past couple of months and I know you are not happy with your own performance level. Also, I want to get you back on track as quickly as possible, so we don't have to have a more difficult conversation next month. I thought you and I could agree to some key things (dials, appointments, proposals, etc.) in order to create a quick turnaround. Once we agree, can you just send me a quick email detailing the items we agreed to? This way I can help keep you on track as the month progresses."

Assuming your rep recognizes the square deal laid squarely before them, you may then begin the negotiation! Do you recall what I said in an earlier chapter about trying to sell a pro? This is where that art form comes into play. Sure, you've softened them up (so to speak), but you are ultimately attempting to close a deal here...a deal that will keep Mary at her numbers while keeping you from having to fire her. You know what the numbers should be, but you need to get Mary to tell you what the numbers should be. If the correct number is eight appointments per week, yet she contends the number is six, you must get her to eight. You do this by knowing how to sell someone who (in theory) sells for a living.

"Mary, we could do six, but let me ask you a question. You have been averaging six per week and you have missed your target for two consecutive months. Knowing that we are trying to get you back on track for a winning month, do you think you can win with that number?"

After doing this dance for a while, you should get your rep to a point where she believes in the numbers; after all, *she* came up with them...didn't she? Sell the pro. This also makes it easier to manage Mary as time goes by. You can simply present her with the email and make statements to the effect of, "Mary, you ran six appointments last week. My concern is that this was not the goal you set for yourself. What can I do to help you hit your goal of eight?"

This Soft Plan approach did, in fact, help my leaders overcome their fear. It also served its purpose of letting people know what was coming. Whether you decide to do this or not, I would choose one of these processes, or a modified version, and stick with it!

Performance Improvement Plans (PIPs)

I did not invent the PIP, but I am certainly a master of its correct, effective execution. When you fail to provide performance feedback, people tend to stay past their welcome, so to speak. When you try to fire them, you realize it is going to be an issue. So, then you burden them with an impossible plan whose metrics they will never fulfill, therefore allowing you to "justifiably" fire them.

The cycle continues in perpetuity. You make your next hire, they make it or they don't, and, again, you implement the monolithic plan to ensure that person is no longer with the company in X number of months.

Congratulations! Your PIPs are now useless, as everyone recognizes that being placed on a plan indicates only that they must now start looking for another job. *You should never use a plan to fire someone.* That is the behavior of a weak leader. <u>Use the PIP strictly to correct unproductive behaviors!</u>

I once had two leaders in my employ present to a group on this topic, which all my teams followed to the letter. They performed an analysis of four sales groups (ours among them). My teams exhibited, by far, the highest usage of PIPs in the company. The difference was in the results our PIPs yielded. Of those reps who were at some point placed on plan within our sales teams, 85% were liberated from the PIP's constraints and went on to become highly productive sales professionals. The other three groups analyzed were revealed to have produced opposite results. Fewer plans had been issued, but 90% of those placed on PIP within those teams were either subsequently fired or left of their own accord. Remember, PIPs should be used for rehabilitation, not termination. Had those other teams operated with that principle in mind, their retention might not have suffered so egregiously.

People want feedback, they really do, and most know when they are doing poorly. They sit around idly wondering if/when they will be terminated. Taking that into account, you owe it to your people to provide them with both clarity and peace of mind. I cannot tell you how many times I would present someone with a PIP, only to have them respond along the line of, "Thank you for giving me this. I really thought you were going to fire me." Trust me: They know they are doing poorly. It is your job to help them understand why and put them back on a path to winning.

The other thing to remember about PIPs is what we talked about in Chapter I. That being the concept that people *really do try to do the best job they can.* For this reason, PIPs need to be a road map toward success. They must be fleshed out with detailed information which will enable people to incrementally exceed their professional obligations. A PIP requiring nothing more than meeting one's quota is not much of a PIP at all. You can be fairly certain if they knew how to do that, they would have already done so!

Below is an example of a Stage One PIP. It is rather basic in nature, but serves as a useful template.

May 15, 2018

Mary,

In an effort to be a clear mirror to you, it is important that I make you aware in writing of some concerns regarding your recent job performance. As we have been discussing, you have fallen behind in attaining your quota responsibility for the past three months. I know we met last month in an effort to turn things around, but you have fallen behind again. As a reminder the expectations of the job are _____ per month/quarter/yr. You are currently at XX% against quota. As a result, here are some basic things we have agreed to:

8 appointments with new prospects per week – You have been struggling to bring in new business. Focusing on new prospects will enable you to add new business to your existing base and should help you in closing the quota gap.

30 new blueprints per week – To find new prospects, we must first identify who these prospects are through the blueprinting process. As a reminder, a blueprint is a contact name who is a decision maker, their direct phone number, email, company name, and number of direct reports.

Sales Methodology/Process – We have also determined that you do not have a strong command of the sales process. As a result, you will need to be prepared each Friday at noon with a role-play scenario covering one of your actual accounts. We will work together to ensure that you have internalized the sales call process and that you are implementing this in your business.

Relationship Building – We have also determined that this is an area of opportunity for you. Building strong relationships will aid you in growing your business and securing longer term opportunities. As a result, these sub-components are necessary:

- 2 client lunches per week
- 1 client dinner per week
- 2 client entertainment opportunities per week (golf, networking opportunity, etc)

As a reminder, your responsibility in this job is to increment quota each month by XX$$. Implementing the items listed above will go a long way in helping you to get back on track. I believe in you and I believe you can win. I am here to help and support you through this process, so please reach out to me should you have any questions or concerns.

Regards,

Will Emmons

_____
Employee Signature

At the completion of the month, you will need to assess the rep's performance in direct relation to the PIP's requirements. My process makes use of a simple decision tree. Nobody is removed from their PIP after a single successful month; however, if they perform well, they would not progress to Stage Two. To come off plan entirely, they need two consecutive months of performance. The reasoning is rather intuitive: A demonstrated trend of recovery is indicative of corrected behavior, whereas a single good month could be attributable to a single favorable deal. I don't care about a single number. I care about trends. If the trends are positive, I know that we are moving in the right direction. One month is not a trend.

The chart below (figure 4-a) illustrates this point still further. Regardless of where in the PIP process a rep finds themselves, two months of *consecutive* performance is key. This is as likely to happen in the second month of a soft plan as it is in the second month of a hard PIP. And, yes—I have employed many reps who seem to essentially live on plan. One, specifically, inhabited his PIP for the better part of two calendar years (seventeen months, in total)! He would constantly porpoise—crushing one month, bombing the next. He finally extricated himself from the plan's constraints, which warranted a good deal of notice on the part of his team and myself. But, three months later, he found himself once again on a much-needed PIP. Not a bad performer, just a very inconsistent one.

Figure 4-a

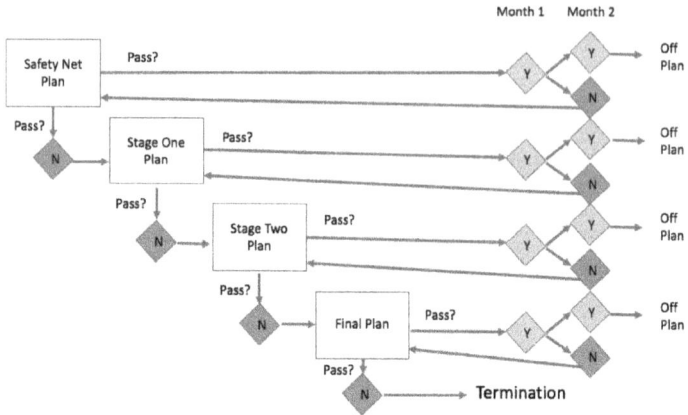

Final Plans

Final PIPs are serious business. They are the culmination of considerable effort put forth by both the rep and their manager. Nobody likes to fire an employee, and (of course) no employee likes to be fired. I have seen people pull things out even at this late stage, but usually it happens earlier in the process. The best advice I can offer when you find yourself here is this: Don't compromise. The numbers are the numbers. By this point, you have likely given them every opportunity to turn things around; if they simply cannot get it done, then it is better for all to begin termination proceedings. Also, remember that not all sales jobs are created equally. The firing of a given rep is not proof positive that said rep is inherently a lacking sales professional. It does mean, however, that this one was not a fit for the company. Tell them that!

Back to the structuring of your PIP.

One essential block of verbiage to include in any final PIP document is as follows: "Failure to meet these expectations will lead to further disciplinary actions up to and including termination." Again, you can also verbalize this, but the recipient needs to see it in writing for the significance to be fully comprehended. This wording achieves the impact necessary for your seriousness to rightly resonate. Also, when I get to this point, I make it clear that all items on the list must be achieved. One of five will not cut it here. To determine the exact wording, you may want to consult your HR department, as they often have required language for final stage disciplinary communications.

Here is a sample document for the final plan. The tone is necessarily different.

The Stage Two Plan would be somewhere between the Stage One and the Final.

Date: May 1, 2018
To: Employee Name
From: Manager Name
Subject: Final Warning Performance Improvement Plan

Per our discussion today, Tuesday, May 1, 2018, you are officially on a final performance improvement plan. This plan will be measured through May 31, 2018. To clearly define the situation you are in:
- You have missed quota for the last five consecutive months
- You are currently $XX behind quota
- You are currently XX% of plan
- You must make up $XX in revenue between now and the end of the year just to get back to quota.

Below is an outline of the expectations and goals that need to be met over the next 30 days:
1) Meet your incremental revenue target, which is $XX,XXX per month

2) Secure your monthly invoicing target of $XX,XXX.

3) Set 10 appointments per week

4) Complete 8 appointments

5) Close a minimum of 3 deals

6) Maintain a positive attitude in the office

During this time, you and I will be meeting on a weekly basis to discuss your progress. Please prepare a summary of your progress for my review prior to our meetings.

Each of these items is independent of the others. This means you must achieve each to prove your ability to continue in this role. If at any time you fail to show immediate and sustained improvement in your performance, or if you fail to meet any of the performance expectations listed above, you will be subject to further disciplinary action up to and including termination of employment from _____ (company name).

The terms of this letter are to be kept confidential between the parties involved.

Regards,

Manager Name

(employee signature)

(employee name)

(Date)

Follow the Trends

One of the advantages of leading a larger team is that it limits the degree to which you can interact with your reps on a more intimate level. Personal connections are nearly impossible to cultivate. It sounds like a strange phenomenon to identify as being favorable, but allow me to provide you with an example.

When evaluating the performance of a given team, office, zone, et cetera, I literally **hide the names of the reps** and let the numbers speak for themselves. I look for any trends I can find: %-to-quota, previous three months' quota attainment figures, retention trends, product-mix sold, appointments, dials, you name it.

There are two things that concern me not at all as I move through this exercise. The first is where they are in relation to their year-to-date numbers. They could be riding high at 1000% of plan or clinging to life at a paltry 10%. I don't care about that...*yet.* Second is the rep's name. This helps me with consistency. Whether you realize it or not, you will make exceptions for certain people. Sometimes consciously, oftentimes not. To harbor biases and favoritisms of one sort or another is to be human—nothing more, nothing less.

When it comes to PIPs, one rank truth I constantly sell to my leaders is the importance of looking at trends rather than year-to-date performance. The reason this is critical is because an essential aspect of your job is to catch people *before* they've already fallen. When you wait until someone falls below quota, it may be too late. Conversely, if you catch a rep who is currently above plan but trending downwards, you buy them more time...which in our field is hugely valuable, even priceless. You also keep from sabotaging your own performance. As a leader, you are likely judged on the performance of your group. So why would you delay taking action until your rep is mired in a deficit, thereby burdening you with the same struggle?

Figure 4-B illustrates this in a clearer visual way. When I tell a leader that they should put the sales professional indicated below on a plan in March, I almost always will (and do) endure pushback. If the leader were looking at the trend data, there would almost certainly be no pushback. Sadly, if I told a leader to put this person on a PIP in June, there would be zero resistance. Why is that the case? The trend is unchanged. Simply stated, the outcome has finally caught up to the trend. In March, the outcome is positive, so it is easy to overlook the trends. Trends will, 99% of the time, correctly forecast an outcome.

Figure 4 - B

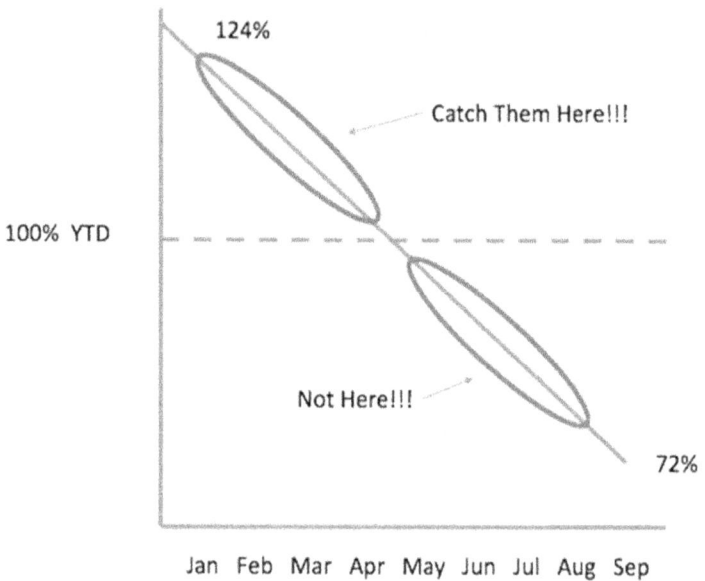

Here I will share with you a real-world example taken from my own time as a leader. I had a rep who started the year above January's quota, but within the first couple of months, the downward trend began to materialize. I spoke to this rep's leader and encouraged them to utilize a PIP in getting them back on track. The sales leader pushed back, essentially arguing that this person was winning and would, therefore, not benefit from the accountability measures of a PIP. In response, I did what I do very well: I gathered my data. Here were the facts as of the end of April:

1)   This rep had fallen short of their monthly

incremental revenue quota for three consecutive months

2)   Their invoicing trend was negative during those three consecutive months

3)   I knew, based on simple arithmetic, this rep would soon fall below quota, even if they started hitting their monthly number, within thirty-sixty days' time.

4)   Furthermore, this person was averaging 20% of the required appointment dialing activity

5)   Lastly, the rep had averaged a meager 3.5 meetings per week, though the quota was more than twice that (8)

The manager took no action, despite insisting she would do so. The results were indeed catastrophic. By the time she took a serious approach to the problem, the rep's sales figures had deteriorated as follows:

1)   78% of plan

2)   318K short of the revenue plan

3)   Rep got killed on his comp. Just as his manager placed him on a PIP, he quit.

The rep may have been shortsighted in managing his activity, but even he recognized this as an insurmountable wall to overcome. I reached out to inquire as to why he was leaving. He told me he had known he was in trouble since the Feb/Mar timeframe but didn't know how to reverse the trend. Essentially, he expressed his wish that someone would have helped him. His leader's own insecurities came at the expense of a solid rep, along with 318K in negative revenue, which seriously impacted that leader's quota number, and thus her compensation. It was a lesson hard-learned.

Chapter V:
Hiring, Revisited

AS A LEADER, YOU SHOULD ALWAYS BE INTERVIEWING. I used to keep a board in my office with the names of candidates, in priority order, who would take over in the event I had an individual who transitioned out of the business (voluntarily or not). One day, I received a school teacher's resume, one who had only a few months' recruiting experience. She in no way aligned with the profile I needed. I was looking for five-plus years of consultative selling experience, at a minimum. I obviously discarded the resume.

And then it began.

Miriam implemented perhaps the most impressive "Get Past The 'No'" campaign I have ever encountered. She began calling me, texting me, and emailing me. I would plainly tell her she was not a fit, yet it somehow bolstered her resolve—she would one day land a job with me, and she would push even harder. She called me so much that my wife thought I was cheating on her. I finally gave in and granted Miriam her interview.

I live in Dallas, Texas, where it very rarely snows, but as Fate would have it, on the day of Miriam's interview, it snowed. A lot! Dallas is not equipped to handle snow on the roads, so even a little of it renders them impassable...for everyone except Miriam, that is. She called me from the office and said she was there. "How?" was my incredulous response.

We rescheduled the interview, and she came in to meet with me. She was great. Enthusiastic, wielding a contagious smile, eager and willing to learn. Unfortunately, she was not a fit, so I told her "No" again. Big mistake. The second barrage began. I thought she was persistent before, but this was next-level stuff. I don't know how many calls and texts went by before I finally caved, but I did. I literally called her to say, "If you promise never to call me again and to be as persistent with your customers as you were with me, I will hire you.". She agreed.

If I could have cloned Miriam ten, twenty, thirty times, I would have been incredibly wealthy. She was amazing. To this day, I kick myself for the months I let escape me by not hiring her. That unqualified school teacher went on to great things, culminating in winning the National Account Executive of the year. She was, to the say the least, a complete badass. What this taught me was that I needed to be interviewing for drive, for gas in the tank. I can teach a lot of things, but I cannot teach what she had. Nobody can!

The question I am most often asked is, "What types of people do you look for when hiring?" To do it justice, my response needs to be broken down into several categories. These include: 1. What I look for, 2. The red flags I know to take seriously, and 3. My absolute "No" criteria. Any interview worth a damn is literally a sales pitches duel. You are selling them on why they should choose you (or the company); they are selling you on why you should choose them. Sales people are necessarily good at this, so your job is to detect the inconsistencies, half-truths, and outright lies which will almost certainly populate their every response to your questions. Expose them to the light of your scrutiny and determine whether or not you have the mental/professional bandwidth to absorb them into your team framework.

For the sake of context, I will note here that I have led teams of the following types:

> Sales teams who both managed existing business and were responsible for new sales growth
> Hunter teams charged *strictly* with selling to new customers
> Farming teams focused solely on renewing and growing existing customers
> Pure SaaS teams
> Overlay SaaS teams
> Inside sales teams
> Outside sales teams
> Enterprise/national account teams
> Small/mid-market sales teams
> Operations teams
> Finance teams

Now that you have an idea as to the sizable spectrum of team-types for which I have recruited, let's explore at some length the lessons I have gleaned in doing so (in no particular order).

1) It takes all kinds – If you will forgive the cliché, this one is simply too apt to be ignored. I have worked with some odd birds. And while I may not have wanted to hang out with them on a personal level, they were highly successful in their jobs. The lesson here is yet another (apt) cliché: Don't judge a book by its cover, nor a person by their idiosyncrasies. In today's schools, bullying has been highlighted and measures put in place to prevent it. Bullying has no place in schools, or in business.

2) An individual's background is not always the most important consideration from a hiring perspective. You will recall my having hired both a zipper salesman and a school teacher into sales roles. Both would go on to win the National Account Executive of the year, though not concurrently, of course. Both were among the most consistent of the company's performers.

When I hired the zipper salesperson, I was in the process of telling him he was not a fit as well when he abruptly cut me off. "Look at your zipper. What does it say?" I said, "YKK.". He responded, "I sold that zipper.". He convinced me that selling zippers was the hardest sales job in the country, and if he had been successful doing that, then hawking our wares would be a breeze. Once properly developed, his prediction would prove correct. He had what Miriam had...gas.

A few learnings from these and other examples:

1) I started telling everyone "No." If they could not sell themselves into the job, I didn't hire them. Some of my peers openly disagreed with this philosophy. It was, in fact, my strategy...and it worked. Take it or leave it.

2) I looked for people with internal drive, or "gas in the tank" as I often put it. People can be taught the industry; drive, however, is unteachable. It is either there or it is not; once gone, it is difficult to reclaim. Later, I will elaborate on this

at greater length in relation to the "rags to rags in three generations" maxim.

3) I have hired people from the big, household-name SaaS companies. These people are always articulate and savvy in the execution of their craft. It is, after all, how they got there in the first place. As a rule, I now steer clear of these types of people. Hear out my reasoning:

a. Watch out for "We," that oft-employed pronoun. In these large SaaS companies, there is usually *one true salesperson* per account—the person who legitimately cracks the first deal open. There is a subsequent host of salespeople who then flood into the breach. It works like this: Deal gets sold, implementation sales team is contacted (they make the call or are simply brought in). This is followed by the ancillary product sales teams who also ride the coattails of that initial salesperson. When interviewing, many of those SaaS souls cannot help but use "We" early and often, a sure sign their "sales" were largely participatory efforts. There is a place for that, but not in a true hunting environment.

b. It's one thing to call the CIO of a given company on behalf of Oracle or SAP. It is another to call in on behalf of Wilco SaaS, LLC. I want people who have had to fight and scrap. I need people who know how to get that first meeting based on the application of skill, not on the strength of a brand name.

c. I never had the luxury of allowing people to be unproductive for months on end. Some of the larger SaaS companies provide their people with very long runways in the form of twelve- to eighteen-month sales cycles. They can afford to do so; I never could. I needed hungry people whose sales activity was governed by a sense of urgency.

d. SaaS sales professionals from big brand names invariably enjoy high (*very* high) base pays. Again, I've never had the luxury of paying my reps small fortunes to keep their bills paid while we allow two summers to pass between deal closings. And in truth, if I did have that luxury, I still do not want people who can live comfortably on a handsome base pay. I want people who <u>must</u> perform and do so consistently. Sales comp plans are exactly that—compensation plans. They should not be on a bonus plan.

Speaking of which, let's here define one of the sales community's most essential terms, courtesy of Merriam Webster's online dictionary [https://www.merriam-webster.com/dictionary/bonus]:

Definition of bonus—

:something in addition to what is expected or strictly due: such as

a :money or an equivalent given in addition to an employee's usual compensation b :*a premium (as of stock) given by a corporation to a purchaser of its securities, to a promoter, or to an employee*

c :*a government payment to war veterans*

d :*a sum in excess of salary given to an athlete for signing with a team*

A well-designed and properly implemented compensation plan will require that those who operate within its parameters perform consistently to receive their desired compensation. Furthermore, such a plan should allow for the possibility of over-production and a desirably financial upside for those who do, in fact, over-produce.

4) A contributor worth her salt will understand her compensation plan inside and out; she will also know how to reap the utmost from it. Whenever a sales professional in my employ is unable to articulate the specifics of their compensation plan, I regard that as a definitive yellow flag. It should go without saying that there are some people who are simply not sufficiently intelligent to engage with and understand any compensation plan (aside from a flat hourly wage, perhaps). That may be the case, but you should nevertheless spend time exploring the depths of your reps' compensation plan knowledge.

5) If you would like to know with certainty that a potential hire did indeed make the President's Club, inquire as to the plan's specific details.

"What qualifying factors were in place, and how many people qualified each year?"

"For which trips, in particular, did you qualify?"

"Where were they held...Oh I love that place, what hotel did you stay in?"

"I have been on lots of company trips and it seems like we always enjoyed such cool activities. Did you do any cool activities?"

"And the dinners we had were always amazing. I am always curious about different and unique places, anything really great that you did there that you   would   recommend?"

6) I am always interested in digging into the way a sales professional acquired and ultimately sold into their account(s). I start with asking about their largest deal. Let's say the total contract value was a half-million dollars. I immediately follow-up by asking how much of that existed prior to the contract being signed (purpose is to find out if they upsold existing business or were responsible for every dollar. An account already sitting at 475K before reaching 500K is not very exciting). This typically determines if I am dealing with a hunter or with a farmer. It also provides a reality check where the individual's self-awareness is concerned. Next, I need to know *why* the customer bought. Can the sales professional adequately convey the value proposition of whatever it was they were selling? Also, are they a conceptual and value-based sales person or a feature benefit sales person? Can they reliably tether the needs of a given client to the specific product they are charged with selling? I also inquire as to whom they sold the solution (obviously looking for executive level sales vs. procurement or low-level gatekeepers). I ask how they secured the meeting. This helps me determine

if they truly did the work of getting in front of the client, or simply followed the lead of another.

7) C-levels – Everyone says they have them...few people really do. Ask for two references who can and are willing to be called on behalf of your interviewee. Ask how many they met with in the previous year. Good sales pros possessing this skill-set will know the answer. It's not a deal-killer, but knowing as much will provide you with a crucial understanding as to the interviewee's broader capabilities.

8) Require them to perform a pitch. Provide them with some information—just enough to be dangerous—and have them pitch to you as though you are a client. You will witness firsthand their level of preparation, along with how they have sold in the past.

9) Meet them several times and in different places. I like to do an early morning, a midday, and one meeting over a drink. I recommend you observe and engage with people in a plurality of environments. If someone is a little on the unstable side, that much will be revealed at some point across that spectrum of settings and contexts.

10)   Referrals – It is an oft-repeated maxim that referrals are the best source of hires.

They have been among my very worst!

Don't get me wrong, they are valuable; but I will tell you here and now to proceed with caution. The mistake I have made (more than once, admittedly) was that I was not as thorough in the interview process **because** they were referred by someone I trusted. As a result, I overlooked essential tells as to the referral's quality. People refer others in the interest of helping a friend...or a friend of a friend. They don't refer them because they know the job inside and out, nor because they have vetted the person and know them to be an ideal fit. I now see to a few screening measures:

    a. I ask the referring party why, specifically, they feel this person to be a good fit. The answers are sometimes frightening, and often unintentionally comical.

    b. I subject them to the same process as all others.

    c. I involve additional people in the process, as they keep me cognizant of my blind   spots.

11)   Tenure with previous employers – This one is something most of you have heard before, but it's worth stating a few things here.

    a. If an interviewee was employed with a company for a long time, then followed that tenure up with brief stays at a few other places, I won't hold that against them. When an employee has been with a company for a considerable stretch, it's usually (though not invariably) due to the company's culture. Some don't realize how important that factor is until it's behind them, so ask both about this *and* if you think your company might satisfy the same needs. In doing so, you may find someone who will stick around. You don't want your team to become a pit stop for professionals in transit. Speaking of which...

b. ...if hiring someone away from a company with which they have been employed for a long time, you might be little more than the first stop of several before they find their new home. Make certain yours is truly the best cultural fit.

c. When someone arrives at your doorstep with a string of two-year stretches behind them, you'd best not waste your time. Whether they simply can't sell, don't get along well with others, or suffer from severe wanderlust, there is typically a reason worth identifying.

12)   Experience means nothing. This is not so much a warning as it is a maxim to bear in mind post-hire. What often gets leaders in trouble is making assumptions about a new hire's experience. Assuming the ten-year veteran you just hired knows the basics of *your* sales process will create problems for   the   both   of   you.

The assumption is as follows: They were previously successful, so they *must know your sales process.* No need to re-teach them how your people dial, how you run a sales call, et cetera. I learned early that requiring everyone (regardless of their experience) to undergo the same training is not only good policy, it is essential. When I realize someone is acquainted with my teachings, we could move on more quickly; if they are not getting it, I slow down to ensure they understand the content I need them to know.

13)   If you interview someone who says they are looking for something else because their boss doesn't _____ (appreciate them, develop them, like them, whatever) RUN! You are just the next person in line for this person to blame for their myriad inadequacies. If you listen to nothing else, <u>take my advice on this one</u>. Such individuals are caustic and will prove themselves a cancer. It took me three rounds with this to finally learn the lesson. All three of them were the hard way. When recalling their respective interviews, all three spoke the above passage verbatim.

14)   *"It's not my decision, but your own."* When I finally reach the point of knowing I am going to make a hire, I bring that individual back in for a final discussion. I let them know that, at this phase in the process, the decision is not mine, but theirs. Here is my basic talk track:

"Sarah, I am comfortable in thinking that you can be successful here. At this stage of the process, however, I am not the decision maker—*you* are. I am going to give you a computer and a phone. I am going to give you a base salary and commission plan. I am going to offer you a good health benefits plan, a car allowance, development, and support. What I am going to ask in return is that you make XX dials per week; that you meet with eight people per week; that you conduct three demos per week; that you add five new opportunities into your funnel each month; that you close $XXX,XXX in new business each month/ $X,XXX,XXX each year. Lastly, and most importantly, I am going to ask that you invest in developing yourself and learning the product(s) in the first three months. This will require a lot of time both at work and at home.

So, you see, you know what the job is. You know what my expectations are, and you know what you will get in return. You also know (because you discussed it) that I will hold you accountable to all these things. If you are willing to sign up for that, I am ready to move forward. Don't feel like you have to provide me with your answer today. It's a big decision and I really want you to make sure you are willing to sign up for all of this as it *is* the expectation."

An interesting thing happens here: Things get real (so to speak). People are hearing how hard they are going to have to work; sometimes they hear things that scare them. Some opt out. Some won't opt out, but they start to negotiate. This tells you a lot about the person, most of it important. They may have passed the interview with flying colors, but this might literally be the first time they indicate they are not willing to do the activity—the push-ups and sit-ups—of the job. They are showing they don't have the requisite gas in the tank. It is a red flag—dig in.

A resume says quite a bit.

You can (and often should) eliminate wholly irrelevant candidates right off the bat in carefully reviewing a resume. For instance, you'll recall my reservations about job-hopping sales professionals, correct? Let the resume communicate as much and shorten the stack considerably. You'll know who is worth at least contacting from a shrewd review of their career history, education, et cetera. And if your recruiters are doing right by you, the weeding out process should not be overly time-consuming. If not, set up a brief conversation with the recruiters and blueprint your ideal candidate(s). A bit of work on this front and you'll find yourself with a solid bench of talent from which to pluck promising interviewees.

This is mostly self-explanatory and serves mostly as a lead-in to an anecdote regarding a referral nightmare I once endured...and lived to recount. And here it is:

The kid was the son of a senior executive's friend (the friend was a highly successful executive himself). What better referral could you hope for? So, I interviewed him less scrupulously than would otherwise have been the case. I hired him with perhaps more optimism than would otherwise have been the case. And I fired him far more quickly than I could have imagined. The reason? He was lazy, entitled, and a terrible hire. The fault was as much mine as his. I took the quality of the referral for granted and should not have done so.

I would have had better luck with a solid recruiter and a decent stack of screened resumes. Less exciting than a "surefire" referral, but far more reliable a hiring channel.

A related piece of advice I'll offer on the hiring topic has everything to do with instinct. Put plainly—trust your gut. Had I trusted my own gut with the executive's friend's kid (sounds like nothing but a red flag as I read that aloud), I would never have made that hire. Conversely, I did in fact trust that very same gut when hiring the former schoolteacher and the energetic zipper salesman. In both cases, my gut overcame my initial doubts. They benefited, I benefited, the company benefited—all thanks to a gut.

Now, having said that, keep your instincts tempered with a modicum of sensitivity to potential warning signs and a few clues as to what you might be in for with different types of hires. Speaking of which...

...Type of Hires: (Note: This is a largely sales-centric section, but its lessons are broadly applicable)

1. Work/Life   Balance   Type

These individuals can come from any walk of life. These are the ones who want to know about the office hours, the travel expectations, and the PTO policy. I have had some highly successful Work/Life Balance people on my teams. There is literally nothing wrong with this hire. You just need to understand a few of the potential frustrations and be willing to deal with them accordingly. They are often motivated to sell, provided the selling takes place strictly between the hours of 8:00 and 5:00. Travel is often a challenge, and trainings that take place outside the standard workday might be out of the question.

This is entirely your call.

If you feel the person sitting across the interviewing table is sufficiently competent to satisfy a sales quota within a tightly governed schedule, go ahead and make the hire. As I said, they tend to be motivated (with obvious exceptions). However, if your gut tells you that personal obligations are likely to interfere with professional responsibilities, it might be best to yield to your instincts. Used correctly, you can leverage their desire for this balance   to   lead   them   individually.

2. Accumulate as Much Cash as Possible Type

In theory, this is your ideal hire. And, on average, that may well be the case. The hungry, ambitious type who would gladly take on the challenge of selling milk to the lactose intolerant provided there is a handsome payoff on the other side of that challenging sale. What could possibly go wrong?

Well, for one, these types are often characterized by a mercenary streak. They'll gladly jump ship for higher paychecks two storefronts down the street. Loyalty is frequently absent the heart of the money-driven; loyalty to anything other than cash, that is.

Nevertheless, even NFL teams are known to take on a skilled free agent if doing so is likely to secure them a spot in the playoffs. Sure, that brilliant linebacker might be playing for the enemy next fall, but your franchise certainly shined while he was in your ranks. Measure the needs of your team, of your office, of yourself. If it makes sense to bring on a mercenary for the sake of driving revenue through the ceiling, then do so. If not, don't.

And, yes, the gut will do the rest, if you choose to hear it out.

3. Home Office Type

You're fated to encounter a lot of these. "I'm *much* more productive when working from home." The truth is, many are. The truth is, many aren't. And as you know, not every position is compatible with the Home Office Type. Inside Sales is governed by a set of guidelines quite different from those of its Outside counterpart. Even so, many Outside reps are still expected to make regular appearances in the office. This one is tricky and extremely dependent upon the nature of your business, the flexibility (or the reverse) of your company policies, your sense of the interviewee from a discipline and credibility standpoint, et cetera.

Suffice it to say that your instincts will go a long way toward deciding if this type is suitable for your team dynamic. Press them hard on their reasoning, on their history with working remotely, and on their openness to being in the office as often as is necessary.

4. Streetfighter Type

I knew a kid in one of my field offices who simply embodied the term "sales." He was first in the office, the last to leave, took client calls on the weekends while golfing, and was hugely profitable due to the low expenses he incurred in closing new business. His direct boss encouraged the team to travel, but this guy closed more deals over the phone than any two reps could achieve in three outside sales meetings.

His success was not a product of talent. There were far more naturally gifted sales professionals in my zone at the time, but most of these were (are) lazy and couldn't stomach more than a dozen dials a day. The streetfighter made that many before his first sip of coffee. He fought for every cent, earned a promotion a year for over half a decade, and encouraged his colleagues to do their best by simply embodying the hallmarks of smash-mouth, rough-and-tumble, in-the-trenches selling.

If your gut tells you the interviewee is a streetfighter (and you'll know it), make that hire. They're rare, typically quite loyal, and need very little oversight. They may require more upfront training than one of your more gifted hotshots; but once they have the product down, it's down for good...and they're off to the   races.

A single Streetfighter Type on the payroll could amount to the revenue cornerstone of a team, an office,   even   a   zone.   Make   that   hire.

5. Walking   on   Air   Type

These people always have me feeling conflicted. Not because they don't bring in any cash. They almost always do. But because I know (I *know*) they could bring in more. But the Walking on Air Type recognizes the talent within themselves and gets by as close to 100% as they can manage without missing their   tee   time...at   noon...on   a   Wednesday.

I know at least one of these individuals who could have been sitting at 200% by year's end if he had embraced the Streetfighter mentality for even a single quarter. But he didn't. For this guy, making the President's Club by finishing at 100.067% was perfectly acceptable. To me, it was, and it wasn't. I could hardly scold a rep for doing his job, but I wished he had tapped more aggressively into his talent.

He wasn't my hire, but I can tell you this: I would have recognized his personality type immediately. You will need to acquire that ability. Now, I'm not going to tell you not to hire a Walking on Air Type. They will be solid contributors. But be ready to go prematurely grey as they cut it close month after month, quarter after quarter. And ready yourself for a host of excuses as to why they can't make it to that team training, or to that dialing contest, or to the office at 8:00 at least once each week.

The best example of this I can think of is a guy I used to equate with Neo from *The Matrix*, particularly as he is toward the end of that film. You'll recall his effortlessly achieved victory over the once-indomitable agents, I trust. That was him, while the Streetfighter is more similar to the still-nascent Neo who, earlier in the film, tries stubbornly to overcome the far stronger Agent Smith in a subway tunnel. He wins...but barely, and he fought hard for every punch.

It's business. As a leader, you take the good with the bad. Just make sure you know ahead of time what exactly you're taking (hiring).

6. Semi-Entitled Type

It would not be life if an older generation didn't quite grasp the confusing culture of the generations that follow them. A lot of younger interviewees are going to walk through that front door expecting a great deal more than you ever did, especially at that age. The question here is: "Can I train this person?" If so, perhaps their entitlement will in time wane. Competitive atmospheres tend to separate young minds from their myopic worldviews. Not always, but often. Do your best to determine the <u>potential</u> of an interviewee. Remember—as a sales leader, your job is to educate and condition reps for a brutal marketplace.

Many a young soul may be categorically unequipped to withstand the transition; many a young soul is subconsciously hungry for a challenge. Wrench that hunger into the forefront of their mind and fashion a professional in your own image.

Oh, and be ready for growing pains.

The graduation from entitled mentality to informed responsibility will be neither swift nor devoid of pain. Hey, you wanted to lead, right? So, lead. Most human beings are trainable, and the overwhelming majority want to be led.

Above all, learn to hone your instincts and trust them always. It will take time, you will experience moments of doubt, and you will make bad hires. You must, as a leader, distill useful lessons from the agony of error. Your continued success hinges on as much.

Chapter VI:
Focus (Full Stop)

AFTER SPENDING TWO YEARS working in Asia, I assumed leadership responsibility over the European chapter of my company's international business, and a major problem became immediately apparent: My predecessors had radically shifted focus away from our centerpiece products and toward newer, more glamorous ones which renewed at a cripplingly low rate. What I effectively inherited was a series of teams whose respective sales reps were incentivized to sell a plurality of products, the details of which were largely lost upon them. They had a broad menu at their disposal but could scarcely tell me a thing about any one dish. This was alarming, to say the least. Not to mention, much of what they were selling simply did not yield adequate results for our clients to justify a renewal. And who could blame them? They were being pitched complex products by reps inadequately equipped to explain what was being offered.

The work of cleaning this up was time-consuming, it was taxing, and it was outright necessary. Correct product emphasis was crucial, as was identifying the right people for the right jobs to implement my ambitious corrective strategy. I also needed to author and implement the correct processes for the purposes of plan pull-through. We executed on this plan relentlessly and achieved our goals.

So how exactly did I go about this?

First, I measured our product suite on a market-by-market basis. Unlike the United States, whose individual states are bound by federal law and operate within the same market framework, the European Union was, at that time, comprised of 28 countries (27, post-Brexit) in a membership system. Each country is governed by and accountable to unique laws surrounding data security and employment; each is beholden to their respective cultures, customs, business sensibilities, corporate climate, et cetera. Failing to take inventory of this pluralistic landscape when attempting to sell within it amounts to corporate negligence and leadership malpractice. I refused to be guilty of either.

So, I did what I knew was necessary—I developed market-specific sales/product strategies. This entailed a careful review of the products being exported to each market, as well as an analysis of the actual demand/need for said products therein. Next, I subjected each product to a localization analysis. Which included, for instance, data security compliance (an important consideration). From there, we were able to quickly determine which products fit most aptly within a given market, and which did not.

What followed was a product-focus matrix, which became something of a bible in my world. Stripped to its bare elements, the matrix provided a deep-dive analysis of each market, each product, and each team within a given market. The last of these was assessed by its sales/product strengths and weaknesses.

Next was the people side of the equation. We became evangelists with respect to the selling of certain products/services, and largely washed our hands of others. This was the goal of the matrix. Operating in accordance with the "bible," we were able to intelligently re-structure the sales team and to align it with our findings in terms of core product viability and ideal retention rates. Elite specialty teams followed, with the goal of constructing new product sales strategies on a market-by-market basis. This organization also allowed us to remove our low-profit/high cost Solutions Architects Teams—which had been necessary in the absence of proper product emphasis—and create highly skilled sales teams in their stead. Waste was eliminated, profits increased.

Our newly focused teams were highly knowledgeable. Their singular talk-tracks allowed them to overcome objections with confidence and competence, a combination which had been entirely absent prior to my implementation of this model.

The last component was alignment of the comp plan. We moved to a model focused on selling the right deal types and deal terms, and away from one-time, short-term, low-profit deals. We did not nail the comp straight out of the gates, but in working with local leaders, we developed the right plans by market to support the growth model.

The results spoke for themselves. Several emerging product teams experienced growth rates exceeding 40%. Every market benefited from the system, and some would enjoy increased YOY profits approaching 30%. We also turned around an unprofitable business suffering from YOY declines in revenue for the previous five years. It is important to bear in mind that this market had suffered from years of consistent decline prior to my arrival.

I am tempted to begin and end this chapter with its title: Focus. After all, if taken as a single word of advice, it stands nicely on its own.

But I have a thing or two more to say on this subject.

It's a word we hear all the time—focus—and whose meaning we're largely certain we understand...until we stop to think about it. The truth is, most of the people with whom I have worked in my day simply can't fully comprehend the meaning of the word, and fewer still are capable of executing in accordance with its implied fundamentals.

Contrary to many misconceptions, focus has nothing to do with stripping people of workplace freedoms or implementing punishments of some sort. Even if such things become side effects of a focus-driven plan, they should not be central to its execution. If they are, then your focus is out of focus.

Let's stop here to better understand the word itself.

The etymology of "focus" is unusual, in that we know it was used in Classical times to denote what we now know as a hearth, but the origin of the term ends there (at least our understanding of it). By Post-Classical times, the term had forked into two separate meanings. In certain contexts, it was used to denote fire; but in mathematics, "focus" indicated a convergence point within a calculation. The shift appears to have been organic and is difficult to trace.

Still, it is a blend of both meanings that characterizes our modern understanding of "focus" when used as a metaphor or in direct reference to a trained and dedicated mindset. We can certainly connect the word to that image of a blazing hearth. After all, focus, like fire, is energy-intensive. But we also intuitively picture a converging of goals, plans, and activities when focusing with rigor.

Ever seen a film where a character's plan or vision begins to slowly come together? Whether we're talking about the *Rocky* training montage or Michael Corleone's systematic "whacking" of his many rivals, the audience is basically witnessing a direct product of intensive focus. An exercise regimen, a scheme, a sequence of events. The specific circumstances don't matter—the characters must be seen focusing on a given outcome for these scenes to resonate with the audience. We relate to both the fire (hearth) and the intersecting of key steps (convergence).

Leaving the film examples behind, let's pivot to one of the most important truths of focus: It is about maximizing one's existing resources, not necessarily seeking out new ones. What you will find in contextualizing focus in this way is that focus truly is a gift. Its proper exercise will allow you to extract far greater value out of what you already have at your disposal. It is what military leaders refer to as a force-multiplier. It is potent, necessary, energizing. And it is within reach. You don't need to wonder where to go about finding it; it's already in you. Harness its power. As a leader, you'll need to summon focus to the forefront of your mind and channel its effects for the benefit of your team.

The results will materialize quickly and noticeably.

Your reps will learn more quickly as your trainings take on a more substantive, enriching, and relevant quality. They will subsequently execute your strategies more adeptly and enthusiastically. And, above all, they will sell more...period.

There is not a successful start-up business in existence that did not benefit from zealous, severe focus in its earliest of days. As an ingredient, it is exactly as essential as is a good idea, a useful service, a marketable product, et cetera. It is equally essential for businesses suffering from slumping sales, heightened competition, and marketplace uncertainty. Absent focus, the start-up will fail; absent focus, the struggling company will not regain its footing.

Okay, so now you know what focus is and why it is important. But, knowing these things, do you find yourself wondering why so many find the adoption and maintenance of a focused mindset so difficult to realize for themselves and others?

Here are some common pitfalls:

Chasing Rabbits:

The term "chasing rabbits" is well-known in the sales space. Being a strong business professional, you abhor the idea of walking away from a deal. The result is that you inevitably pursue every lead to populate your desk, rather than sticking more faithfully to the leads that got you to where you are in the first place. Innovation has its place and should be accounted for in any long-term career planning. But most ideas are destined for the waste basket of corporate history. And the good ones need time to take root, to be vetted, to have their weaknesses exposed. Silo new concepts as they materialize, but don't allow each one to detract you from a successful model.

Remember—there are countless ways to make a buck; not every one of them is worth your time, your energy, your focus. I always tell people, the fact that you *can* make money at something does not mean you *should* make money at it. There is no shortage of rabbit holes in corporate sales. Chase every one of them at your own peril. Learn to distinguish between an idea with strong potential and an idea with strong allure; the two are rarely one and the same. Sometimes, but not often.

Look at the product matrix I explained in the opening of the chapter. When I arrived in Europe, each country was chasing no fewer than 15 products (rabbits). I challenged the leaders in each market to focus (that word again) on no more than four. With a lot of pushback, concern, and apprehension, each of them executed on the plan. Again, the results were extraordinary.

As a leader, you will inevitably find yourself attempting to steer a rep away from a sales cul-de-sac. They will insist they are one flight, one meeting, or one PowerPoint presentation away from closing an enormous deal. And are they? Maybe. But if your instincts tell you the likelihood is slim, or that the rep is myopic in this instance, help them to see things your way. No sense in throwing good time after bad. There is no telling how, specifically, a given "rabbit" scenario will take shape in your world...but know that they will. Learn to distinguish between items worthy of your focus and those worth discarding immediately.

Misaligned Comp Plans:

Too often, comp plans are misaligned and force people to adopt behaviors that disrupt their primary business focus. A friend owned a staffing firm and was struggling to build his consulting practice, though his permanent placements were growing. The problem with this is that permanent placement fees are one-time payments, whereas consulting fees generate recurring revenue, and in the staffing world recurring revenue is king.

My first question, as you might imagine, was about his compensation plan.

"Hey, how are you paying your people? Which services are prioritized in relation to the bonus/commission structure?"

As it turns out, he was paying his people a premium on permanent placement fees. The answer could not have been any clearer: Align the compensation plan with your overarching aims, and the behavior will change immediately. He corrected his comp plan, made some other changes, and got things back on track.

Compensation plans are like an old-school radio. For the millennials and for the generations that follow, I've provided a picture.

With this model, you had to precisely tune the five knobs on the front of the radio to locate the specific radio station for which you were looking. Compensation plans are a lot like this. You may not need five levers (or knobs), but you will typically want multiple components. Here are some examples of different comp buckets or levers you might consider:

Profitability	Money Collected
Deal Size	Invoicing
Deal Volume	Recognized Revenue
Target Account Focus	One-Year, Three-Year, Five-Year (or longer) Contract Terms
Products	Service Contracts Sold

There are countless other factors in play. The key is to think about your business and what you are trying to achieve, and then create the necessary incentives to drive behavior.

A word of caution here: If you provide incentives on something new while removing an incentive, you need to both inspect *and* put new rules in place.

Back to Europe for a moment.

When I arrived, the comp plan was established in large part around one product. This was the office mentioned above, which also had terrible retention rates. The problem was that if a rep wanted to stay whole on comp, they had to figure out how to "position" the product effectively. They knew nobody wanted to buy it, so what did they do? During the renewal period, they went to their customer with the following offer:

"I know you spent €50,000 with me last year on product X. If it's OK with you, I am going to give you product X for €0 this year but will charge you €50,000 for product Y".

Surprisingly, many customers agreed to these terms. Two things resulted. First, the business failed to grow, but the reps were compensated as if the business increased at a high percentage. Second, the following year when renewal season came back around, we were in trouble. Customers had examined their bill. Most had never even implemented product Y, and those that had, did not use it. So, the discussions were as follows:

"We don't really need Product Y. We just want product X".

The problem was that they now associated the value of product X at the values we had been invoicing them for it all year: €0. It was a tough renewal season, and the business suffered greatly.

Lack of Alignment:

You will *never* be successful without proper alignment. Allow me to repeat that.

You will *never* be successful without proper alignment.

Your people (sales reps, leadership team, etc.) need to be very clear on the strategy, the expected end results, and the key areas of focus that will get you there. This means you will have to inspect early and often. If you find any deviation from the expectations, you *must* act immediately. It is up to you to decide how serious the action needs to be, but I can tell you that I do not mess around with this. I might give someone one chance, but if they cannot self-correct, they cannot remain on the team.

This is especially true of your leadership team. Your leaders are a direct extension of you; they have an exponential effect on your capacity for necessary execution. I give my leaders their chance to push back while I am working through my strategies, but once we have all beat things up and a decision is made, there is *zero* variance from the plan unless data dictates we should and we all agree collectively on as much. I have left more than a few leaders in the wake of a successful business turnaround. They were unable to align themselves effectively, so they had to go.

This is how I drive alignment within my teams:

1) Get the people in a room and allow for a debate. I want healthy and spirited debate on the problem, how we got into a given situation, and how we get out of it. I come prepared with my own answers, and I expect feedback on those, as well. I don't care what they think...I care what they *know*. Opinions don't matter. Data does.

2) Once we decide, it is agreed upon. Meaning we may not necessarily agree that the plan is right, but if I am the most senior person, I have listened to the feedback and I have set the path. I then expect everyone to be on the bus. If you are not on my bus, you are not on my team!

3) Again, I must be relentless in checking that everything we decided we would do, everything you signed up to do, is being done...period.

- For sales alignment, I had weekly calls with my SalesForce analyst to learn what was truly happening in each market. Were my hunters staying true to their product sets, were my farmers only working and managing existing accounts, were my SaaS teams staying focused on the singular product focuses?

- For marketing, I had weekly calls with my head of marketing to discuss key metrics and alignment around spend per market, ROI based on spend, profitability by market, and market performance against plan and correlated marketing spend.

- Weekly calls with our head of SaaS implementations to review our agreed-upon metrics around our contracts signed, launch call, production, QA, go live, customer satisfaction with implementation, and areas where implementation needed sales to help remove any bottlenecks.

- Monthly customer care calls to review retention rates, customer trends, needs for additional support, etc.

- Weekly product calls to prioritize the tech queue for each product and market, as well as review upcoming product needs

All of these led into my weekly calls with individual sales leaders, where I would use all this data to ensure alignment was actually in place. Where it was not, I could quickly make adjustments and improvements. Again, sometimes I had to educate, sometimes I had to sell. In some cases, I had to remove.

Lack of Patience:

At one point in my life, unhealthy eating choices and a lack of nutritional/physical discipline left me with more than a few extra pounds to shed. I hired a trainer and we started to develop a plan to get me back on track. I asked how long he thought it would take to achieve my goal. He looked at me and explained that I had not arrived in his gym because of one month of bad habits. They had accumulated over months and years of poor discipline and lack of focus. He explained that getting back on track would also take time. Maybe not years, but certainly six months or more.

Business is no different. A business becomes unhealthy after months and years of poor discipline and lack of focus. Then one day, whether by our own recognition or by the mandate of a new owner or boss, we find ourselves at a crossroads. We are forced to either fix the problem or find another job. So, we analyze the business, identify the areas we will improve upon, and then we execute on the new plan with extreme urgency. Comp plans are aligned, people are being held accountable, and then...nothing.

Relax.

These things take time, as well. I think most new strategies take at least three months for the earliest signs of success to materialize, and probably another three months for the revenue to follow. Just like the example above, it took you a while to get to this point and it is going to take some time to get out of it. I want to stress that you should be measuring along the way,. for indicators or trends showing you are on the right track. If you see a need to make some minor changes, fine; but don't abandon ship. Be urgent, but be realistic.

How do you decide what to focus on?

1) Examine the Data

As I previously mentioned...I don't care what you think. I care what you know. The only way to know is to have the data, so start with exactly that. When you start digging into data, look at everything and look for the best and the worst. You want to identify your greatest strengths and, by extension, your greatest weaknesses. We still care about the things in the middle, so don't ignore those. The point is to maximize your strengths, eliminate your weaknesses, and improve on everything else.

My guess is that you already know what your best and worst products are. There are other things you may not know yet:

    a.   Products – Most/Least Profitable. Highest/Lowest Retention Rate. Shortest/Longest Closing Cycle. Largest/Smallest Deal Sizes. Highest/Lowest Market Share.

    b.   Industries – Most/Least Profitable. Highest/Lowest Retention Rate. Shortest/Longest Closing Cycle. Largest/Smallest Deal Sizes. Highest/Lowest Market Share.

    c.   Geographies - Most/Least Profitable. Highest/Lowest Retention Rate. Shortest/Longest Closing Cycle. Largest/Smallest Deal Sizes. Highest/Lowest Market Share.

    d.   Contract Terms - Most/least profitable. Highest/Lowest Retention Rate. Shortest/Longest Closing Cycle. Largest/Smallest Deal Sizes.

    e.   Customers - Most/Least Profitable. Highest/Lowest Retention Rate. Shortest/Longest Closing Cycle. Largest/Smallest Deal Sizes. Upsell Opportunities?

    f.   Customer Support – Time Spent Per Customer. Time Spent by Customer. Existing SLA's. % of customers where we are underperforming against SLA's/over-performing against SLA's.

There are literally endless things to measure, but get as much as you can.

2) Make some decisions

There are countless ways to spend your time and allocate your resources. For starters, every organization and/or sales office has a veritable "sweet spot" of one sort or another. Let's assume for a moment that a staffing company's Denver office might do exceedingly well with manufacturing and retail. By well, I mean that these two segments are both very profitable, and they make up the majority of this particular office's business. That said, this office only penetrates 5% of each industry. Putting a maximum focus on these two segments and abandoning others might be a reasonable way to get the team focused on driving business in a segment we know we'll perform well in. In this example, we might only allow our people to prospect new business in either retail or manufacturing vertical accounts.

Concentration of customers or *potential* customers might also be an area worthy of proper consideration. Going back to Denver for a moment, let's assume the data told us a different story. We were strong in manufacturing and retail, but also had heavy penetration rates in that market. If that market is definitively saturated, perhaps you turn your attention to Salt Lake City and Santa Fe.

Again, the data will tell you where you need to focus. Your job is to develop the appropriate strategies, create alignment, and execute.

3) Profitability

This is a lesson that needs to be learned and re-learned by even the most seasoned sales managers and senior figures: "Revenue" and "Profit" are not interchangeable terms. The second is invariably fueled by the first, but the first does not necessarily lead to the second. No matter how you ultimately choose to spend the hours in your day, make sure you are always <u>focused</u> on profitability. This goes for deals and reps alike. Some reps sell high-dollar deals from the comfort of their desks, others run up the corporate card with endless travel to secure the occasional renewal. Care to guess which one is profitable?

As for business closed...

...a $1,000,000 deal almost always looks attractive at first glance. Get lost in all those zeroes at your own peril. A seven-figure agreement that ultimately nets out $50,000 is poison. Run from that one, and quickly. This should go without saying, but an unfocused sales manager might sign off on the contract without factoring in the overall +/- of the deal.

Much of this is a judgment call you will need to make after carefully reviewing the numbers. It's always ideal to run such things past a finance professional, especially when you're dealing with larger deal sizes. The bottom line is that you should invariably seize a high-margin opportunity, no matter the size. A $250,000 deal that can be done over the phone with minimal cost, and thus at a high margin to the company, is a great deal. Conversely, a quarter-million-dollar sale that will cost the company $240,000 to properly fulfill is a bit low and should be evaluated against other considerations.

These include upsell potential, heightening of your industry standing, and partnership opportunities. If none of these seem viable, that $10,000 net might not be worth the trouble.

So, that's my take on focus. And if you hope to enjoy sales leadership success, it should be yours, too. I'll re-visit this topic here and there in later chapters, but if you've read this far, you know what you most need to know on the importance of focus. Use that knowledge wisely.

Let's move on.

Chapter VII:
Coaching Trees: Planting a Leadership Forest

Leading Leaders: Pride, Humility, & Lessons from the Trenches

Imparting Knowledge Through Example

NOBODY LIKES TO BE LECTURED TO. Some people enjoy a good lecture, admittedly, but not one among them likes the idea of being singled out for a one-on-one lesson. It's an undeniable truth of our species—being on the receiving end of lecturing, spoken-word instruction is off-putting, regardless of the instruction's legitimacy.

There is no perfect "way" to lead. Some are proven to fail, but success manifests itself in many forms. For better or worse, I believe in leading. Meaning, I like to be out in front. I will outpace, outperform, and I like to flat-out *lead*. A lot of people, given the option, will move with less speed. I want new people in my world to feel like they are always behind, because they usually are. It's not their fault; they simply know what they know. My job (and yours) is to teach them how to quickly assess, gather data, set strategies, implement those strategies, and then measure, measure, and measure still again.

I think a lot of leaders want to lead from behind. Particularly during difficult times, many leaders want to "hide" behind a desk and tell people what to do and how to do it. Unfortunately, it is during such times that people are most seeking wise, skillful, knowledgeable leadership. If they knew how to get off the hill, they would have already done so. When chaos strikes, I strive to be the person everyone looks to. There is comfort that is portrayed from a leader who is in the trenches at times (not all the time, which can itself be detrimental) showing the way. These are the moments when good leaders shine, and when poor ones are likely to wilt. They can demonstrate an ability to lift others up, removing them from harm's way in the process.

But back to teaching and leading methodologies...

Sermonizing, preaching, using the bully pulpit, getting on your soapbox—they all carry with them the faint odor of condescension. People dislike condescension and respond negatively to it. It also doesn't couple overly well with the art of teaching (or coaching). Skillful teaching is typically characterized by both patience and the establishment of rapport between teacher and pupil. This carries forward to the relationship between coach and athlete; and it certainly carries forward to that between sales leader and sales rep.

Don't sermonize to your team, nor to your office, nor to your company. Talk to them often and create with them bonds born of shared struggle. Announce successes in grand style, but let the failures speak for themselves, at least publicly.

You might be thinking, "How can I realize the changes I want made if not by pointing them out?"

I'm not against open communication, and you shouldn't be either. I'm against allowing the spoken word to operate in place of a solid example. You know from earlier in the book that I'm a big believer in candor. The way I get my junior and mid-level leaders to adopt the same mentality is not by telling them to do so...which wouldn't work anyway. I get them to adopt the mentality by inhabiting it myself, showing them what it can achieve, and allowing that example to find purchase within their minds. It's very easy to tell who in a given organization stems from the Emmons Coaching Tree. Not every leader in my orbit adopts my candor to the same extent—personalities differ far too wildly—but the frank communication for which I am known reliably takes root in each of them and, in time, comes to characterize them.

Now imagine a scenario in which I hire an up-and-coming sales manager. Let's call him Todd.

Todd is competent, knowledgeable, and had himself a good run in the sales trenches. He knows his worth, makes no excuses, and represents the company well. He is intelligent, honest, curious, and dependable. But...

...but Todd isn't quite as frank in his communications as I'd prefer, certainly not when dealing with underperforming sales reps. His kind nature prevents him from cutting to the heart of the matter. He fears causing his team members any emotional trauma.

Now, what I am do with Todd? He's a terrific sales manager and does excellent work for the company. The only ingredient absent his leadership recipe is that of candor. Should I just tell him to speak more candidly? If done properly, this could work. In fact, I probably would do that. Something along the lines of, "Great work, Todd, but try infusing your conversations with more candor."

Okay, so that might move the needle a bit. Or he'll take exception to being instructed on how to communicate. It's a weird brand of constructive criticism, and one that often annoys more than anything else.

Where I would experience greater success is in allowing for the power of candor to speak for itself. Perhaps I organize a series of account reviews in Todd's office. Todd will participate to a limited extent, but his reps will largely be answering to me and a few outside leaders. Throughout the process, I exhibit the blunt, honest, ultra-transparent style of feedback for which I am known. The reps respond in that familiar way brought on by candor—with truthful, bullshit-free answers about their accounts.

Over the years, my style has changed tremendously in these instances. I cannot stress enough that people should not walk out of these meetings feeling like they just walked out of an exchange in which they were being rapid fired upon by the enemy. Maybe even having taken a few bullets. They should feel appropriately challenged, but confident that the feedback can be taken back and implemented into action. These are not bullying sessions to prove you are the smartest person in the room. They are development sessions to help people move the needle quicker in the business. There is a *very* fine line!

Todd can witness for himself why a philosophy of candor is so central to my leadership persona. The rest will happen in time. Either way, I did not allow a lecture to operate in place of a strong example. This aspect of leading/coaching should essentially stand as an ongoing challenge, which I'll be covering right now.

Challenging Your Best to Better Themselves

As we just discussed, you must embody the qualities you want others to themselves embrace. This goes for everything from punctuality and appearance to client interactions and sales success. Imagine taking fitness advice from a notorious sloth with virtually no self-discipline. The message is immediately forfeit due to the messenger's lack of credibility. Same goes for sales leadership. If you want your team to dress in accordance with the Mad Men era, terrific; but make sure you are personally attired as well as Don Draper. Want the team to show up at 7:45 to get an early jump on the dials? That's fine. Just make sure you've got a Box o' Joe in the break room at 7:30.

This is a baseline standard of leadership, nothing more. It is the starting point. If you aren't doing these things, you aren't leading, and you may not be fit for leadership at all.

The work of setting a high standard and exceeding it yourself is essential for two reasons: 1. The preservation of morale on your team, and 2. The pushing of your most talented reps to also exceed the standard.

Every team has its shining stars. The rep who can sell in her sleep; the rep whose monumental deal from three quarters past will still be carrying him three quarters later; the rep who can perform half the work (if that) yet somehow produce twice the results (if not more). Talent, by definition, is innate. It cannot be taught or transferred, it cannot be measured or copied, and it is often the enemy of its wielder. It can breed complacency, arrogance, and indifference. It can extinguish the fire of ambition by eliminating the drive necessary for its realization. It can ultimately undermine the greatness created by its very presence.

But none of these possibilities are inevitable.

A good leader will recognize the top talents within their team and create the circumstances most compatible with their strengths. They will also demand as much of them as they can produce. Asking anything less is absurd—the talent never learns its true capabilities, the team fails to maximize a valuable resource, and the leader is failing in one of their overarching responsibilities.

The fact that great athletes don't always make great coaches mirrors the fact that great sales reps don't always make great sales leaders. Acknowledge that truth for what it is and proceed accordingly. If you have a phenomenal sales rep on the payroll, terrific. But don't necessarily assume you have a phenomenal successor and future leader in your midst. You might, you might not.

I have, four times in my career, moved the number one sales rep in my organization to a sales leader position. So far, I am 2-2 when it comes to success with this model. I have promoted many other successful people from producing roles into leadership roles, but I am strictly referring to the best of the best. I can easily explain to you where I went wrong. The two who were successful sought me out. They had achieved success on their own and they were hungry to go to the next level. They wanted to teach others, to develop new talent, and to replicate their success on a larger scale. They wanted to learn new skills, including how to lead. The other two...well, *I* sought *them* out. I sold them on why they should become a leader. I convinced them they would be great and, in turn, would develop carbon copies of themselves. The latter group had no interest in developing. They had no interest in learning to lead. They were selfish, wanted to be liked, and they certainly did not want to adopt my leadership philosophy. That, in a nutshell, is why they failed. None of those attributes were at all detrimental when they were responsible only for themselves; they were, after all, sitting atop the President's Club trip tracker every month. We wanted and needed them there.

The lesson here is that you cannot *make* someone want to be a leader. They either aspire to that or they do not; if they do not, tread lightly in attempting to persuade them otherwise. From my experience, I can assure you the results are often catastrophic (50% of the time, in my case). Not only have you removed your star producer, you will waste months wallowing in low production as other reps decline in their output. You will ultimately remove the leader (likely via demotion) and, upon doing so, witness that person exit the organization. They always leave disgruntled, confused, and mistrusting of you...always.

So, then, how does a leader go about creating new leaders? Read on.

Cultivating your coaching tree is matter of identifying fundamental leadership characteristics in others, observing those characteristics in action, making corrections/suggestions along the way, and subtly guiding your protégé forward. Along the way, you should instill lessons and give shape to the underlying philosophy which will guide your mentee's leadership experience. This patient, responsible, sensitive approach to replicating your own leader mold is manageable and scalable. It also rejects the idea of promoting to leadership based solely on sales success. Doing so might be met with a successful outcome, but not reliably so, as we have seen.

Why is all of this so important? Put simply: Success. When you couch it in variable terminology, it can take on different forms. Some might term it "leadership development." Others refer to as "succession planning." Some call it "executive grooming." These are one and the same.

In my professional experience, HR teams have always managed the corporate succession planning and development factories. They were not terrible in their execution, but the people they produced did not necessarily fit my needs. For that reason, I started (and have invariably maintained) my own group of potential leaders.

I have always sought out people to bring into my world. When conducting quarterly leadership meetings, I was constantly seeking up-and-coming leaders for enlistment into my group, all while developing existing leaders as they continued their own ascent. Because of this, many of my people were plucked for other jobs outside of my area, which was fine with me. In fact, I took (and take) a lot of pride in that fact. My "brag sheet" of those leaders to have been plucked from the Emmons Coaching Tree remains unsurpassed.

One nearly fatal mistake I made, however, taught me a valuable lesson about the importance of this. I was responsible for both enterprise field and mid-market sales teams across the U.S. The mid-market teams were usually in one area, had several line-level managers, and were led by a senior director. In this latter position, I placed one of my people who, for personal reasons, had to step down. This left me with a high-level open position in a critical business area. I was receiving some pressure to promote the next "company superstar" into that role.

Unfortunately, I listened, with extreme consequences.

This "superstar" knew nothing of the core values to which the line-level leaders were accustomed and had not been groomed within my coaching system. Candor was entirely absent, as was accountability. A case of leadership bankruptcy took shape. So severe was the office's dislike for this person that it ultimately imploded. I did draw lessons from the experience, but they were expensive ones. First, I should have promoted someone I could trust to honor and maintain the culture of candor, development, and accountability under which those teams had thrived (read: one of my own people). Second, I should have gone deeper in vetting the candidate to determine the presence (or absence) of those vital attributes. Third, I learned that positive referrals mean nothing until I have properly evaluated the candidate in question. In the end, you've got to trust your gut.

<u>Your Leadership Orbit</u>

Measuring Success Within Your Circle

"Steel sharpens steel," or so the old proverb goes. Surrounding yourself with good people is advisable both socially and professionally. In the corporate world, we don't always have complete say over the individuals with whom we are required to work, travel, collaborate, et cetera. As a leader, however, you have a good deal of control over hiring, firing, and rep swapping. The days of the medieval court are long gone, which means you can't treat people like disposable pawns or engage in outright favoritism. What you *can* (and should) do is create a sales environment in which the right behaviors are rightly rewarded, the wrong ones reprimanded, and the cream can reach the top. In short, you should run your world as a meritocracy.

You don't need to discriminate in any overt manner. The weak links will eventually fall off; the strong ones will strengthen your chain. As that process unfolds, keep an eye open for signs of leadership potential among the best of your inner circle. And be mindful of those who thrive when operating under your guidance, but who may not do as well on their own.

How to Mitigate Dependency

It is inevitable: Many of your top performers will do well as a direct result of your support, your example, and the selling ecosystem you oversee. They may thrive on your energy, they may benefit from the choice accounts your talent has attracted, and they may prefer to reap rewards while avoiding accountability. Whatever the specific circumstances, some reps depend on an established selling framework to achieve success.

The Peter Principle, which states that an individual will eventually be promoted to one level higher than their competency should allow, often comes into play here. From the company's upper echelons, it appears that one of your reps is a sales dynamo. If they can get him into a leadership role, he can replicate his success tenfold.

You know full well that this guy is not suitable for leadership. He's good at taking care of Number One and operating within your system. If asked to lead others, his deficiencies will become apparent within days. How do leaders contend with this reality? How do they encourage growth and independence with those who most need it?

Selfishness & Selflessness: The Incompatible Traits

Success in Sales: A Leadership Non-Indicator

We've touched on it throughout the book: Selfishness and selflessness are mutually exclusive traits, and only the latter is compatible with what it takes to lead well. It is true that selling encourages a modicum of selfishness in all who practice the trade. This is an immutable aspect of the human nature. For a select few (you among them), an innate altruism manages to weather the storm of greed and self-interest while they are themselves in the trenches. What emerges from that storm is an individual with knowledge of sales psychology, practice, and struggle who also carries with them the drive to help others along the way.

Notice I said nothing about this person's level of sales success. Important though it is, it is not essential to the role they are best suited to occupy. I would not advocate promoting a downright lackluster salesperson to a managerial role, but neither would I require that they were the company's top earner. I am looking for a combination of talents and personality characteristics, only one of which is actual sales performance.

Sales is *not* one of those games where the person on top this year was the same as last year. You see it from time to time, but rarely. Besides, selling a large deal that puts someone on top of the score card says nothing at all about that person's leadership potential, as we have discussed. What I look for is consistent performance history. Perhaps a rep has qualified for the President's Club trip three years out of the past five. They might even have consistently ranked in the top 10-15% for the past three years, but never in the top three. I am not going after newbies, nor bottom-feeders. I want people with a little history and a proven track record.

I have seen in many instances where the "Flavor of the Month" gets selected for leadership, and herein lies another cautionary tale.

Take Heather. She started with the company around mid-year. Heather came in and immediately inherited a thriving book of business from her predecessor...who is now also her boss. Heather assumes nominal control of these accounts, which her boss also has an interest in closing. Heather is recognized on every recognition call. Heather is invited to leadership meetings. Heather starts to believe the hype! Uh-oh. Heather gets selected for leadership. Heather starts to teach, but teach what? She didn't really *do* anything, but Heather thinks...no, she *believes* she did. Why?

Well, because we told her she did. Heather was the "Flavor of the Month" and, unfortunately for Heather, that ice cream ultimately melted, as ice cream does when removed from the safety of the freezer! Heather might have been good had we slowed down, worked her into some other accounts to test her strengths while coming to know her weaknesses. Had we afforded those weakness the attention they were due, she could, potentially, have been great. Unfortunately, she was not, and we demoted her. She left disgruntled, confused, and mistrusting. Another potentially good person whose career was compromised by circumstance, by delusion, and by improper development.

Learning from the Sidelines: Why Runners-Up Often Lead/Coach Well

Duane Ludwig is one of the most sought-after striking coaches in the mixed martial arts world. Upon hanging up the gloves, his own MMA record was 21 wins and 14 losses.

Not terrible by any measure, but probably not the sort of record that leads to "Greatest of all Time" talk (though he is a *truly* great fighter). Where Ludwig may very well be among the greatest of all time is in his coaching ability. Countless fighters have sought him out and subsequently seen their performances measurably el.

This is one example of hundreds I could offer. Whether you look at golf, football, or any number of Olympic events, the best coaches often had middling success of their own prior to throwing the whistle (or stopwatch) around their neck. There is probably a psychological angle to this worth exploring, but let's just take it as a hallmark of human experience for the time being.

I've known a great many rock-star sales studs in my day. The type who will spend more time in airport hotels each year than in their own home; the type who will take an emergency sales call on Christmas morning; the type who lives by the rep rankings. These people are gold. They keep the lights on for everyone else. They live to close.

But they can't always lead.

Some of the most admirable and successful sales managers I've personally worked with were, at best, top-10% reps in their own day. Maybe top-5%. Regardless, they were not the rock-stars described above. They lacked either the talent or the ruthlessness...or both; but not the drive. They were observant and they were hardworking. They did what was asked of them and they did it without complaint. And they could often be seen helping others. They were competent and knowledgeable, both of which are essential for solid leadership.

Take, for example, Mike, who always wanted to be in leadership. Every discussion we ever had, he asked me about it, but his performance was never great. It was OK, but not great. He was definitely a B player on the team. We had many discussions, and I laid out a plan for him to earn the right to have a serious discussion about leadership. It was a combination of leading by example, sales performance, and inclusion into my leadership group. Over time, Mike earned the right for the discussion and, eventually, was given a shot.

Not surprisingly, Mike did very well as a leader. He showed a real affinity for the position, and the fact that we slowed the conversation and developed him in key areas prepared him for success. His was one of the best performing teams in the group, which earned him several sequential leadership responsibilities. That is the correct approach to leadership development, and one I hope you will yourself adopt.

Can the Selfish Lead? Can the Selfless Sell?

Those are the questions, aren't they? In a word, yes. There are instances of great (and selfish) salespeople going on to lead thriving teams. And, as I've already acknowledged, many great (and selfless) sales leaders were themselves solid in the trenches. The former is by far rarer than the latter. There are simply too many examples across all industries of Top Gun sales killers who prove unable to impart their skill and talent upon a team. They are mercenary in their instincts, which does not allow for a thoughtful imparting of lessons upon a protégé.

Again, there is no silver bullet here. I am simply providing the reader with my experiences and mistakes in this area. In reference to truly successful sales people, it takes all kinds. This is also true of successful leaders. I believe firmly that the trends identified here are real and worthy of attention.

This analysis should inform your understanding of leadership and its defining characteristics, but it should not operate in place of your own observations. Perhaps when leading a team of your own, you will prove capable of successfully grooming a hotshot sales pro for a management role. Wouldn't that be something? On the other hand, perhaps a goodhearted but average rep of yours will end up being too passive or indecisive to be an effective leader. If either scenario ends up coming to pass, write to me. I am always looking to broaden my horizons and to better understand this elusive topic.

Chapter VIII:
Candor, Loyalty, & Standing Your Ground

<u>Candor: The Essential Leadership Element</u>

What is candor?

MOST OF YOU LIKELY HAVE SOME IDEA as to what "candor" means, even if you wouldn't feel comfortable defining it outright. It's a term I've come to closely cherish over the years, if only because its generally accepted meaning is so frequently associated with my name and professional reputation. For the record, I don't mind at all. Whether the association is made favorably or otherwise, I think it's accurate.

Candor is a rarity these days. It is not absent altogether, but it is often absent where it is most needed.

Have you ever viewed an enjoyable YouTube clip (music video, film trailer, guy falling off deck) only to scroll through a bevy of weirdly hostile comments a little way down the page? It never fails—even the most anodyne of video content will inevitably yield at least some "This sucks!" input from viewers masked in the anonymity afforded them by the Internet. This might meet the definition of "candor" in some circles, but audacity is easy from afar.

My idea of candor is altogether different.

Candor is the telling of hard truths. It is allowing honesty to prevail at every turn. It is cutting through the minutia and getting to the point. When introduced into a new environment, one in which truthfulness has been relegated to second-tier status in favor of polite dishonesty, the result might be a brief drop in morale, but that has not been my experience. What I almost invariably observe is respect and gratitude for the frankness that has been lacking and, by extension, hurting business to one degree or another.

As I have stated before, candor is a tricky thing. There is a fine line between being blunt and being candid. Again, the former is hurtful and devoid of empathy and compassion. The latter is well thought-out transparency, with respect for a person's self-worth and unique circumstances.

I had a sales rep years ago who was reporting into another sales leader, yet wanted to speak with *me* as to why they were not winning. I agreed to the discussion, which she began by asking me why she was not successful. I quickly adjusted the conversation's terms, with her activity as the centerpiece. I first asked, "Debbie, how many appointments did you run last month?" "Six," she said. "What was the expectation?". "Twenty-five," she said. "How many appointments do you have scheduled for this month?". "One, so far," she replied.

Debbie was in a state of delusion. She was asking questions whose answers were already known to her. They were plainly apparent; she just did not want to accept them. So, I nicely asked her to describe the problem as she understood it. She sheepishly answered, "I need more appointments." I verbally agreed but did not want to let her off the hook that easily.

I explained to Debbie that, as a professional at her career level, I should not be speaking with her about dials. I certainly could (and would) let her leader know to monitor this going forward, but holding oneself accountable is a critical function of success. I also explained that she would need to self-correct the harmful behaviors, and that if she failed to do so, a discussion regarding her future in the position would follow. I wanted her to be successful, but what I saw was an obvious lack of effort. Not a lack of ability, nor skill, nor belief. Just a pure lack of effort. She agreed, we ended the call, and Debbie went on to crush her numbers. We never had another discussion regarding lacking effort, though we did discuss her wildly successful year soon thereafter. The lock was lacking effort; the key was candid discussion.

In the long run, nobody benefits from smoke-and-mirrors leadership. Avoiding a difficult conversation with an underperforming sales rep will spare the leader a bit of discomfort for that one day; continued avoidance will see the rep's performance suffer further, which will in turn reflect negatively on the leader. Letting a person know where they stand, good or bad, is always preferable to ignoring essential truths. Not every rep will want to accept damning honesty, but they will almost always come to appreciate it down the road.

How is candid communication best exercised in a sales environment?

Okay, so we've laid a broad groundwork on candor. But how specifically does candor pertain to *your* role in *your* company? How does a sales leader exhibit candid communication in ways both responsible and effective? Is there a wrong way to be professionally honest?

I'll answer the last question first: Yes.

Because candor is often mistaken for simply having no inner monologue, it's important to draw a major distinction here.

Being a candid leader does not give you license to speak every thought that comes to mind, particularly those that might be offensive or otherwise irrelevant to the work of driving revenue. You might find a rep of yours to be a tacky dresser—so what? If it doesn't violate any stated policies, leave it alone. Another rep may be an insufferable Oakland Raiders fan—who cares? So long as he's not barreling into the office on Monday morning with a painted face and plastic armor, forget it.

Obviously, if you feel you have enough rapport with a subordinate to get away with the occasional ribbing, have at it. But don't mistake that for the sort of candor I am espousing in this chapter. Jocularity exists elsewhere on the honesty spectrum, and it does have its place, just not here. And remember that when you are the boss, it's usually not that funny, as your subordinates have to take the joke and rarely feel empowered to give it back.

The sort of candor which has colored my entire sales leadership persona is based strictly on performance evaluation, professional conduct, and my sense of a given person's potential. And it is plainly objective. Plainly.

How objective?

I will tell you here and now that personal affinity counts for nothing in my book, at least not in comparison to sales success. The same goes for general indifference. I could have absolutely no interest in getting to know a sales rep in my zone, fine; but if that rep is doing fantastically well and routinely hitting their numbers, I'll be the first to publicly sing their praises.

Now flip the coin over.

I could have golfed ten times with a rep, attended their birthday dinner, and sent them both Christmas and Hanukkah cards, but the moment I realize that person is falling behind or not achieving what they should be achieving, I will share with them candid feedback and provide the same clarity around expectations of performance I would give to anyone else. I am, above all things, consistent with everyone...to a fault.

Ask any sales professional who's ever seen me operate. This is a hallmark of my character and should be for you as well. I like my friends and have made many throughout my decades in sales, but I believe in being just and fair without exception. Without even having to think too hard on it, I can produce a list of ten reps who I scarcely knew on a personal level but whose hard work and commitment to meeting their respective quotas earned them my highest public praise. They did well and deserved to be acknowledged for it, regardless of how well I did or didn't know them personally.

I could just as quickly produce a list of buddies who got a bit too comfortable, grew a little soft, and eventually became unprofitable. If you ask them how I responded to as much, the answers will be remarkably consistent. I made clear my distaste for their lack of performance in a way that was commensurate with the offense. And with good reason. First, whatever my shortcomings in life, I don't ever want to be accused of favoritism. Loyalty is one thing (and it's a *good* thing), but blatantly overlooking a subordinate's poor performance based on personal feelings, that's inexcusable. And if I were to ever be accused of giving favor, it would only be to those who were successful. Lose success and you lose favor. Second, in the long run, you're only hurting your own business. Keep covering for the slacker's poor work and eventually your office, region, or company starts taking a hit. And why? Just so the two of you would still be friends during happy hour? In my experience, when you let the hammer drop, you find out really quickly who your real friends were all along. The good ones will recognize their professional shortfalls for what they are, correct course as necessary, and respect you all the more for holding their feet to the fire.

Your friendship will either remain intact or grow stronger all around. The bad ones will grow defensive, play the friendship card, and either fail to correct course or do so begrudgingly. This process plays out reliably and provides a good deal of needed clarity.

Remember: You never want to become too entrenched with one office or one group. That only yields complacency and is often accompanied by accusations of favoritism.

This urge is really difficult in settings in which you manage a single group of individual producers. You are with them every day. You know about their entire life, and it is really hard to stay on the leader side of the line and not cross over to the friend side. You may be able to do both, but I never was very good at it, so I always kept my distance on the "friend" front. I tried to avoid being the therapist, the shoulder to cry on, or the scapegoat. I focused on consistency in my development and treatment of my teams, and I delivered the same message to all people, regardless of the circumstances.

How is candor typically received?

Okay, reader, here goes.

Candor is often received badly.

There you have it. I encourage you to read on, but you've just read the section's most important string of words: Candor...is often... received...badly.

Your job as a leader is to brace for uncomfortable moments, the moments brought on by having to deliver hard truths in direct language. If you're reading this book, I'm guessing it's not because you had some vision of leadership as a retirement hammock. I certainly hope not; it's anything but a hammock. You are destined to be pressed from above for dollars and from below for your time and energy. And guess what—the candor needs to move down *and* up the ladder.

That's right, cupcake, you aren't just shoveling crap down to the bottom-feeders. When the boss (and everybody has one) asks about last month's revenue drop, steel your resolve and confront the question with dignity. If an account took a nosedive for reasons beyond your control, say so. If an account took a nosedive because the assigned rep screwed up, say so. If you have no idea why an account took a nosedive, say so—but then come up with some answers.

This is one way to ensure your form of candor is not mistaken for bullying. Though not necessarily easy, it is certainly *easier* to speak hard truths when the recipient sits lower than you on the food chain. But if you are known for sticking to your guns no matter the title opposite you, then that quality becomes a virtue.

And don't forget the clients. This applies to them as well. Have you ever seen a rep or a manager with a reputation for being a hard-ass who becomes a well-behaved lapdog when speaking with an important client? It's a pitiful sight, isn't it? Aside from the discomfort we all feel when observing an obvious façade, it also calls into question that person's mettle. Are they only tough among friends? Is it all an act?

Some of the hardest conversations I've ever had have been with clients. When I was in the moment, most (if not all) of the difficulty could have been mitigated if I had sugarcoated the facts or avoided them entirely. But in doing so, I would have compromised my integrity and rendered my reputation subject to suspicion. Plus, the hard truths wouldn't have been changed or addressed; they simply would have been sidestepped for a time. The problem is, failing to confront challenges still leaves you with those challenges—they're simply afforded more time to fester.

At one point, I ran a Bay Area HCM SaaS business. When I took this entity over, I was coming in on the heels of a series of bad decisions. We were not failing across the entire customer base, but we were failing in specific niche areas of the business. I needed to gain credibility with our clients (both former and current), so I did the only thing I have ever known to do. I told everyone the truth. I explained to them the mistakes that had been made over the past few years. I laid out what the plan was to correct these issues in the months ahead. I empathized with their experiences and I asked them to hold me accountable to delivering on the things I said I was going to do. Partly due to my lack of industry knowledge, but mostly due to my talk track—I never talked about the product. I talked about their experiences. I spoke about their needs. I also spoke about me and my commitments. It was not lip service. We delivered. We won back old customers and we retained the existing base. It was a longer road than I had anticipated in the beginning, but I think the path to success would have been much longer and harder had I tried to spin-sell my way out of the hole we were in.

Okay, with that important anecdote having been shared, let's return to the leader/rep dynamic.

The major obstacle to candid discourse is the fact that we are human beings. We are social creatures and are, in most cases, sensitive to the feelings of others. This becomes a major hindrance when, for instance, an underperforming rep happens also to be likable, and polite, and a single parent, and trying her best, and a regular contributor of doughnuts to the breakroom, or any number of things.

We don't exactly welcome the idea of confronting such an underperformer when we correctly anticipate the reaction will be emotional. But, and I'll stress this throughout, you're doing the underperformer (and yourself) zero favors by avoiding the matter at hand. The rep is making less money than is possible, your office numbers are taking a hit, and it looks like this person is getting a pass for bringing in delicious doughnuts every other Wednesday morning.

Now, if you've already laid the groundwork for a team, office, region, or zone predicated on honesty and transparency, these conversations are easier to have. If not, they may seem as though they've come out of nowhere. Let's fork the concept two ways.

Scenario A: Honesty/Transparency Groundwork is in Place

Sales Manager: "Hey, Kate, can we speak for a moment?"

Kate: "Yeah, of course."

SM: "Kate, you're an excellent asset on the team and you bring a lot of terrific energy to our mission."

Kate: "Thank you."

SM: "You likely knew this was coming, your numbers have been slipping for nearly three months. I know your second-largest account cut their spend by half. We talked about that and I agree that there wasn't much you could do. However, I haven't seen the right sort of effort from you in working to cover that loss and grow elsewhere."

Kate: [nodding] "You're right. I was in a good place this time last year with my top three clients. I took it and them for granted...got a bit too comfortable."

SM: "Which is understandable, Kate. We're all prone to resting on our laurels. But I would be failing you and the team in not mentioning this as I'm doing now. We're not in PIP territory, yet, but it's not out of the question."

Kate: "That's more than fair."

SM: "Show me what I know you're capable of this next month. Produce some new revenue, add new contacts, and pull yourself out of this rut."

Kate: "I'm on this. And thank you for being straight with me."

SM: "That's how we do it here."

Scenario B: Honesty/Transparency Groundwork Not in Place

SM: "Hey, Kate, can we speak for a moment?"

Kate: "Yeah, of course."

SM: "Kate, you're an excellent asset on the team and you bring a lot of terrific energy to our mission."

Kate: "Am I in trouble?"

SM: "Not exactly, but we do need to discuss your numbers."

Kate: "What does that mean? I'm trying my best. You know my second biggest client cut its spend in half."

SM: "Yes, I know. But that was last quarter, and you haven't put anything new on the board."

Kate: "So what do you want me to do? I thought I was doing okay. I bring doughnuts every Wednesday and my clients love me."

SM: "Those things aside, you're still not doing what you were hired to do: To meet or exceed your quota."

Kate: "Have you talked to every rep about their numbers? Because I know that Samantha and James didn't hit their quota last month."

SM: "This isn't about them. Let me worry about the team's collective number. I have to—"

Kate: "It just seems like I'm being singled out."

SM: "Not at all. You don't know what I do or don't say to your colleagues."

Kate: "I know. But this just came out of nowhere. We've never talked about my performance before, and you've always just told me I'm doing a good job."

SM: "You're right, I have...and maybe I failed you in doing so."

Now, this is obviously a stylized and simplified set of scenarios, but they do illustrate the fundamental difference between a sales environment characterized by candor and one characterized by false optimism or performance neglect. In the first scenario, Kate was accustomed to receiving objective reviews of her professional quality. She accepted the criticism and elected to make changes where necessary. In the second scenario, Kate was accustomed to being told nice things; the idea of being held to account for lacking sales was unthinkable. She grew defensive and rightly pointed out that accountability wasn't really a part of the office formula.

I won't argue that matters are ever so black-and-white in practice, but these responses are generally accurate. Keep candor at the center of your leadership philosophy/practice, enjoy mature and reasoned responses to legitimate criticisms; marginalize candor altogether, expect to face emotional backlash when addressing important concerns.

Now I will necessarily contradict myself. I have as many examples of people finding calm and relief from my candid discussions as I have of those who felt uncomfortable with them. Take Amanda. When I met her, she was in serious trouble from a performance standpoint. Her previous leader did her no favors and, in fact, never gave her any feedback...good or bad. When we met for the first time, she would literally avoid eye contact with me. It was a rough first meeting, but I saw something in her: An unwavering will to succeed. She, I believed, simply had never been given the chance to do so. So, I shared a few things with her in that first encounter, but nothing major.

During our second meeting, the eye contact dilemma had not abated, so toward the end of the discussion, I simply asked her what was wrong. I asked if she was afraid of me or if she simply had an eye contact phobia. I got a little chuckle, but it did not last long. Finally, with tears in her eyes, she looked up at me and said something to the effect that nobody ever told her anything, good or bad. She shared her dedication to the job and to the company, and then ended with, "I just know that I am not doing well, and I am scared to death that you are going to fire me."

I smiled and calmly explained to her my methodology. I let her know that I never fire people. People fire themselves. I let her know that I communicate honestly and often. I let her know that, if I believed we were on a poor path, I would let her know. I explained I would provide her with a "soft plan" as a phase one step, a first-level plan as a stage two, a second-level plan as a stage three, and a final plan as a stage four (four consecutive months during which to self-correct). I explained that my goal was always singularly focused: Getting people to win. I explained that, at every point, she would dictate her own ability to get off plan or stay on plan. And, last, that she would have complete control of her destiny and her ultimate success in the company. I got a few more tears, then her lips stiffened...and then she soared.

So that covers candor at a fairly high level. From here, we should look at loyalty and explore how it is best distinguished from favoritism...

...and how candor still belongs in the equation.

~~~

Loyalty: The Perennial Dividend

How is loyalty earned?

Among the many worthy things in life which can't be given and should never be asked for, loyalty is somewhere near the top of the heap. Like trust, friendship, and reputation, loyalty has a way of materializing at its own pace. And once it is achieved, there's little doubt of its being deserved. Rarely does anyone reflect upon someone to whom they are loyal and think, "Well, that was a bit rushed." If that thought process has any standing at all, it calls into question the loyalty felt in the first place.

No, a feeling of loyalty stems from some combination of time and a fair assessment of character. A new acquaintance may be plainly moral, eminently intelligent, and impossibly hardworking, thereby suggesting that loyalty to and/or from this person might be in the cards. But some quantity of time is first necessary to ensure the recipe is compatible with your own interpersonal ingredients.

Conversely, a new acquaintance may be more of a closed book, an unknown quantity, a tad reserved. They seem nice enough, but you can't get a good read. A year or so later, this acquaintance shows you some entirely unexpected kindness and, having also never wronged you, thereby earns a modicum of loyalty.

There are infinite pathways to the destination that is loyalty, and no two are exactly alike. Some friends have known your loyalty from early on, others achieved it over the course of years. Some earned it by way of selflessness, others by simply proving themselves dependable under the right circumstances. Loyalty is elusive, it is impossible to manufacture, it is difficult to unravel, and it is essential to the social fabric of human experience.

I take loyalty very seriously.

And I should. And so should you. Loyalty is the most valuable currency in any setting designed to capitalize on self-interest. Sales encourages a certain degree of selfishness. Being a little selfish has driven many reps to the top and elevated their leaders in the process. A dose of selfish behavior will often spur a sale that might otherwise never have been realized.

Now, imagine injecting something as intangible as loyalty into an environment of that sort.

Loyalty isn't a base salary, nor a bonus check, and certainly not a company trip to paradise. What loyalty is, however, is a promise of support and camaraderie when thick turns to thin. It is mutual, it is valuable, and it is the glue of countless human enterprises and institutions.

Prior to writing this book, I never really thought much about loyalty. It was not until after surveying some former members from various teams I had led that I came to understand how loyal they, in fact, were. It was literally the one thing they all touched on. Each story was unique in how loyalty came to be solidified, but the themes were almost identical.

Those former team members shared the common ground conveyed below:

1)   Candor played a tremendous role in fostering loyalty. They trusted me because they knew I would always tell them the truth about where they stood. When I said things were going to happen, they did; and when I said they would not happen, they didn't. They were all highly successful. According to them, this was because they spent less time worrying about what I was thinking and if they would be fired. They spent more time thinking about maximizing the business, developing their people, and winning.

2)   Trust was yet another characteristic that fostered loyalty. I always had their back. They were allowed to screw up. They were allowed to fail. I didn't protect them in an unhealthy way. I didn't allow them to hide things. I just taught them how to embrace accountability when things did not go well, and how to leverage their momentum when they were on top. My team members were promoted...again and again.

3)   They earned it, no doubt, but I was also their greatest champion. I *never* tried to hold back one of my people to serve my own interests. They all knew this and benefited from it at different times.

4)   We had fun together. In 2009, we were getting our teeth kicked in by the Great Recession. We were all getting beat down and needed to do some bonding...to blow off some steam. From lavish retreats and incredible restaurants, we had been reduced to travel bans and hot dogs. So, early that summer, I rented a house on a lake for $1000. I took my grill, grabbed food, and I towed my boat out. We

had a blast. We talked about ways to keep positive in tough times. We formulated unique strategies to help our teams find success. We did all those things; but mostly we blew off a lot of steam, laughed, goofed off, and bonded like never before. That trip became an annual ritual.

5)   I walked a fine line between the friend/no-friend zone. I always wanted to be respected first and liked second (maybe third). Even though I had closer relationships with some over others, the feedback, transparency, and accountability were non-discriminate. We built great teams and had great success as a result. People won, and people made a *lot* of money. Above all else, this yields loyalty. I have seen the troops turn on the cool guy so many times. People want to have fun, but most prefer success over office friendships.

6)   You had to pay to play. This is not a story of participation ribbons. This was a great company, and this was a great job, but there was one rule: You had to be successful to be able to partake of the good stuff. If you were not successful (following ample feedback, of course) you had to go. Simple as that. The A players thrived, the B players strived to turn into A players, and the C players got moved out.

A key point, and one I hope you'll bear in mind forever, is that loyalty should never trump good judgment, it should never trespass on your objectivity, and it should never impair your instincts. Think back to earlier in the chapter—I have sincerely praised those I barely know and have roundly upbraided those with whom I am personally close. Good leadership requires as much, as does being a good person.

Loyalty is not a pair of blinders, nor a pair of handcuffs. It is an obligation dependent upon the merits and worthiness of those who enjoy it. Which brings us to the question of maintaining loyalty.

How is loyalty maintained?

I won't argue that loyalty is easier to earn than to maintain. That is almost certainly not the case. The initial earning is the highest hurdle to overcome. But the maintaining of loyalty is itself comprised of a series of hurdles. Begin to clip a few along the way, or sidestep them entirely, and your right to loyalty begins to suffer as a result.

Feelings of loyalty are best understood as a wordless conversation. A series of favorable or worthy actions and tacit acknowledgements of those actions will keep the loyalty well brimming. But a series of missteps along the way, particularly brought on by negligence or laziness, begin to siphon that loyalty well.

Along the loyalty super highway there are many exit ramps, but the on-ramps are few and far between. For some, the on-ramp is non-existent. Consistency is always critical to me.

In sales and in leadership, I tend to exhibit loyalty generously, but I am not averse to withdrawing it. Screw up in some manner that reflects poorly on me or the company, and I'd be a fool to regard our relationship as unchanged. Betray my trust or that of your colleagues; I'll close the loyalty door once and for all.

Barring those rare instances, however, your loyalty should carry with it considerable significance, especially as a leader. It should be recognized as a commodity; one hard to earn and comparably hard to keep. It should assure those who possess it that their struggle is your struggle, and that so long as their work is beyond reproach, you are in their corner.

But do not be fickle. If you have committed yourself to backing a colleague, see it through.

Is fragile loyalty *true* loyalty?

That last sentence is intentionally plaintive. The reason is that loyalty is often cheapened by being too easily cast aside when the going gets tough; which is to say, it may never have been loyalty at all.

Be careful not to mistake fondness for loyalty, nor professional proximity for the necessary framework of a mutually loyal relationship. Or do so, but with the knowledge that any real support is unlikely to materialize from such places.

When loyalty is sincere and predicated upon respect and meaningful shared experiences, it does not allow for any sense of doubt to creep in. But when it lacks those undergirding elements, an essence of tenuousness tends to color its place within your mind. Like great art, you know it when you see it—even if you don't always know why.

Candor and loyalty should operate on parallel and occasionally intersecting lanes within your psyche. In allowing them to do so, you will inevitably reach a leadership crossroads. I can't tell you how exactly it will take shape, and I won't pretend to know the outcome, nor your fate. But I can assure you that in adhering to a code of candid discourse and professional loyalty, you will one day be forced to test your mettle in unforeseeable ways.

Take it from me...

When to Fight: The Importance of Backing Your People

"Fire Him, You'll Have to Fire Me" – A Case Study

It sounds like something out of a midday soap opera, but it was my reality...*twice*. In my late thirties, I was one of the company's "old timers." Our average employees were low/mid-twenty-somethings. By many accounts, I was still a "kid," but I was leading people who were, in some cases, first-time leaders. These leaders were young, aggressive, and really young...and young. As I have already stated, they were also very successful. Success does not excuse bad behavior, illegal behavior, or a wide range of _____ behaviors that we could expand further upon. I worked hard to coach my team through challenging situations, but a couple of times I simply could not be there. Make no mistake, when things happened where someone broke laws, infringed on the rights of others in the workforce, or put the company in peril, I was fast and first to fire. When they did really stupid stuff short of these things, I went to bat for my people. Twice it got so intense I threw my own neck on the line. The individuals for whom I put my own livelihood at risk have gone on to be extremely successful. Most importantly, they have owned their mistakes and now are leading and teaching others how to avoid those shortfalls.

Placing Loyalty Above Self-Interest

You are a budding leader, or one looking to grow. For that reason, above all others, I'll say it again: *It is no longer about you.* Understand that there are levels of loyalty on the human menu. I would never argue that a brand-new rep of yours deserves the same level of loyalty as a lifelong friend.

But the brand-new rep does deserve *some* loyalty. Consider it a draw against commission. It's a loyalty derived from the trust they've placed in you to lead them well; it's a loyalty derived from your desire to set a good precedent. And in many cases, the rep may have little to no power of their own. Could be a fresh college graduate with no connections, no knowledge of the industry, no friends in the company. The selflessness requisite in any leadership role requires that you recognize vulnerability when you see it and insert yourself where necessary to moderate it.

That process requires a loyalty advance, of sorts, and one which stands to yield considerable dividends if received and rightly reciprocated by its beneficiary. As I said, there are levels. In any social scenario, loyalty is due nobody until it is earned. When you are wearing the horns of power, loyalty to those in your employ is an essential leadership tenet.

Separating self-interest from the equation is impossible. We all want to do well for ourselves and for our families. But leadership requires a more dynamic, cerebral approach to those aims. You must learn to help others prosper in order that you might prosper yourself. Knowing when to fight, how to go about it, and for what reason is par for the leadership course. Clients will be clients, quotas will be quotas, and the economy will bustle along as it always has. But in the workings of those gears and levers, your willingness to take a stand should be recognized and respected.

The time to start establishing that reputation is now.

Chapter IX:
Sales, International:
Quotas, Diplomacy, and
Navigating Customs

AFTER SPENDING MY ENTIRE ADULT LIFE selling and leading sales teams in North America, I had a conversation with my CEO at the time. I asked him a simple question: "Where do you see me going from here?". He looked at me and, to my surprise, said, "You know, I have been thinking that you could really be an asset for us in the international business.". I was speechless. After all, I was a kid from Texas. I had lived a few places in the U.S., but I always made my way back home to Texas. He explained that he felt like my process could benefit a struggling business. His sole concern? My communication style, of course.

Admittedly, I also had concerns about that. I knew I had grown up a lot and that my communication style was much improved, but did I have the demeanor needed to adequately manage the complexities of the international businesses I would soon be leading?

I experienced many moments of self-doubt regarding this and several other areas. When you take an international assignment, you take on two jobs. The first is the job itself, of course. The second is that of company ambassador. In leadership, people watch your every move and use you as a litmus test to determine what is and is not appropriate. In the international business (at least ours) you are in many ways *the* connection to the "mothership.".

I have seen more examples of this role done poorly than well, but those who master it enjoy great success. Those who get lost in their international assignments, which are indeed too good to be true at times, often neglect the ambassadorial aspect of the position. Put simply, these jobs require maturity, tact, self-control, and a level of restraint many do not possess. In other instances, they may possess those attributes but ultimately suppress them when it matters most.

No one ever told me this, but I quickly learned it...thankfully not the hard way.

I had always romanticized the idea of one day jet-setting around the world like some much less attractive version of James Bond (minus the exciting shootouts and gorgeous women). Sales would be close to the same, but...different. It didn't happen right away. In fact, it wasn't until about a year and a half later that the topic once again came up, and at first it was centered on my running our operations in China and starting up locations throughout northern Asia.

It was everything you might imagine. Which means I had no idea what I was doing. I think we were all a little naïve regarding the start-up aspect of the job. I was to launch new SaaS operations using U.S. SaaS products with little-to-no localization. Sounds simple, right?

Not so much.

To provide you with perspective, the first page you loaded on our SaaS product asked a few questions. First was the date, which was in the "mm/dd/year" format...which only exists in the U.S. Next was a Social Security number field. No explanation needed.

When I started, our page-load times were north of ninety seconds. I don't remember exactly, but I am pretty sure even in the AOL dial-up days, page-loads were faster than that. This was painful. We literally high-fived the day we got it below sixty seconds. As you can imagine, demos were challenging to the point of being impractical.

Nonetheless, I had a job to do and I set out to do it. Luckily, I was soon given responsibility for all of Asia. We had offices in Shanghai, Hong Kong, Tokyo, Ho Chi Minh City, Hanoi, Delhi, Mumbai, Singapore, Kuala Lumpur, and Jakarta. I was metaphorically drinking out of a firehose, as the saying goes.

Only humans sell (you don't see any other animal cold-calling) and the art is as old as civilization. Items designed and built/manufactured in Colorado can be sold and used in Morocco, just as goods made in Ancient Greece could find markets in Ancient Egypt. People need things, use things, buy things, trade things, and sell things from one corner of the globe to the other.

Which is not to say that selling is without its challenges.

Trade has always been difficult. Trading locally means dealing with local competitors. Trading over long distances means dealing with...well, with long distances. In ancient times, that often meant braving the elements, steering clear of thieves, and being without your family for weeks, months, or even years. These days, long-distance selling can be done with a telephone and a Skype account, but still requires a good deal of travel (take it from me). At least these days the only thievery you will likely come across is an insane baggage fee and whatever hijinks the airlines are up to.

The fact is, we are consumers. Look past your basic needs (shelter, food, water, comfort) and you'll see we have an eye for a lot of stuff we really don't need, stuff we are often interested in importing from far-off places. For that reason alone, international trade dates back thousands of years.

One thing about doing business in foreign lands is that you often need an interpreter, someone charged with helping to create an exchange of ideas, knowledge, and even sales pitches between individuals who might have no other effective way of understanding each other. The importance of their work goes beyond translating a word from Language A into its Language B version. That is important, but it is only part of what makes a good interpreter valuable to business professionals who rely on them.

Interpreters are also expected to educate people from far-off countries about what is and is not allowed in the host country. What to do and when; how to do what you're going to do; which member of a gathering should be addressed; which members should receive exaggerated courtesies, et cetera.

There's an old saying: "If you want to know who rules over you, simply find out who you are not allowed to criticize." Interpreters were necessary to identify people above criticism for visitors who might not have a clue.

In some ways, that old saying is still relevant. I'll explain.

Overseas and long-distance trading have always been around, but the idea of companies setting up full-fledged shops in foreign countries is arguably new. Even if you can find some example of that in the financial and manufacturing industries, the idea of taking a software sales operation overseas is something else altogether. Software is hard enough to sell without the problems of a language or culture barrier.

That's exactly what the software company in which I held several senior leadership positions did: They set up shop *all over the world*. I learned *a lot* during that time. For one, it's never a bad idea to know who you can't criticize—that way you know who to track down for a real decision.

There's a lot to cover in this chapter, but I'll start with this: Nobody cares what you did in the United States. If you see yourself one day leading an overseas sales team, you will likely find yourself in front of a group of people trying to explain something and will, intentionally or not, utter the words, "In the U.S. we did..." It is difficult to avoid drawing on your own perspective and background. But know that as soon as you say those words, the people looking back at you are mostly thinking, and some will actually say, "Nobody cares what you did in the United States."

My deal with employees overseas was always this: I won't say "In the U.S. we did..." if you won't say, "That won't work here." We'll get back to that soon.

Here's why nobody cares: The fact is, your U.S.-based sales success was achieved with different products, and under different employment laws, housed within a different culture, constrained by different government regulations, responding to different economic conditions/pricing pressures, and dealing with different competitive forces. The context is entirely, yes, different.

The United States is a relatively young country. European and Asian countries had many centuries to develop countless cultures, languages, and customs. But America came about pretty quickly over the course of around eight generations (from the earliest days of colonization to the American Revolutionary War). Language, religion, custom, law, cultural identity, political foundation, technological development—all of this was tossed into one national recipe. The result was the United States of America.

Europe was born of a hundred recipes over thousands of years, which left them with a collection of unique countries such as Germany, France, Spain, Italy, and Poland, to name a handful. England belongs in there, of course (we're borrowing their language for this book, after all) but their situation is unlike the others in many ways.

The point is, selling across borders in Europe is in no way similar to selling across state lines in America. Pennsylvanians and Texans may seem distinctive on the surface, but they can at least be expected to speak the same language and follow the same Federal laws. That is not true of, for example, the Portuguese and the Croatians.

No matter what company you work for, you never want to make the mistake of saying, "We are going to start a European operation or an Asian operation." What you will do is start operations in Sweden or Spain or Japan or Singapore. Each of these countries has their own set of governing laws, their own language, and their own customs and beliefs. Assuming you can treat any of these as a collective group is both naïve and ignorant. Yet, time and time again, U.S.-based organizations make this mistake.

Germany stands out as a prime example of this, due to its extremely stringent data security and protection laws. Products easily sold across the rest of Europe are extremely challenging to move into the German market because of these laws. This is also why so many U.S.-based companies have both tried and failed in their hopes of monetizing Germany's large economy.

Even companies like Walmart, which have enjoyed global dominance, struggle to crack the code on operating in Germany. Walmart, which at one time operated 85 stores in Germany, eventually pulled out entirely. In fact, there is a litany of large brand names that have enjoyed enormous success in the U.S. market, only to try and fail in the German market, all owed to the combination of cultural misunderstanding, under-anticipation of difficult regulatory restrictions, and general naïveté.

The same holds true for China and Japan, where cultural barriers to entry and regulations are difficult to overcome—arguably even more so than in Germany. Companies like Google, eBay, Home Depot, and a long list of others have first struggled and then failed in these markets. The laws in China, to name one example, are built to favor the Chinese, which makes it difficult for any foreign company to win or even marginally succeed.

In my own experience there, we were forced, based on Chinese law, to enter into a joint venture. What this essentially means is that we could not own our company outright. We had to basically gift 51% to a Chinese national. I cannot comment on this person or how we came to work with him. I also cannot comment on our experience with him. What I can tell you is that having the right JV partner in China will make or break you.

We broke.

These laws are not enforced for all companies or industries, but ours was one forced into this arrangement, which ultimately ended poorly for us.

Even Minnesota-based U.S. retail behemoth Target failed miserably when it tried to take advantage of the Canadian economy just a few hundred miles to its north. In a very short amount of time, Target lost billions, then tucked tail and ran back across the border after failing miserably. The failure was for slightly different reasons than the others, but the commonality was an overconfidence (bordering on arrogance) about its go-to-market strategy.

In the "Land Down Under," Starbucks went in guns blazing. It opened over eighty locations, only to find that locals loved their coffee from...well, from *other locals*. As a result, Starbucks closed nearly all those locations, but have since made a modest comeback. According to their corporate site, they now have thirty-six stores in Australia.

Buying philosophies also differ from country to country. In the example above, regarding Walmart, the two areas cited for their failure were 1. the greeters, and 2. minimal produce availability. The German culture is one I enjoy quite a bit. But make no mistake: the Germans are a very distinctive people in terms of their cultural norms.

In the U.S., we smile when saying hello or goodbye, but this runs contrary to German culture. In Germany, the Walmart greeter basically creeped people out! They did not want to be approached in the stores, let alone with a smile. Something else you will notice when taking a stroll through the old town in Munich is the large outdoor farmers' market. Fresh, naturally organic fruits, vegetables, and flowers are abundant. Consumers were turned off by the comparatively small produce selections crammed onto Walmart's shelves. We are used to this in the U.S.; however, the Germans did not take to this, and eighty-five store closures later, Walmart was no more. Germany was to Walmart as Canada was to Target. The mighty can always fall.

Walmart also found it difficult to operate in the way to which it was accustomed when dealing with local producers and employees. In the U.S., they buy in bulk and put downward price pressure on suppliers. German consumers and laws do not support this idea. Similarly, Walmart works diligently to drive down wages and keep labor unions out. Again, this is not a practice supported by the employment laws or the culturally accepted norms of the German people. As I learned in my own experiences, terminating an employee in Germany is, in fact, a negotiation.

First, the employee must basically agree to be terminated, and *then* you must negotiate a severance. There are norms for what is typical, but there are no absolutes. This, as you can imagine, must have been very difficult for Walmart.

I think you get the point, but when looking at an international strategy, you have to take this into consideration for any of the nearly two hundred possible countries you are considering moving into. It's not seven continents (assuming Antarctica is in play). It's nearly two hundred countries.

Okay, so now you know that custom/cultural differences are a fixture in the realm of international business. But you already knew that. Here's one thing you might not have known: It doesn't matter. Not really, anyway.

Here's what I mean.

You're going to hear it from time to time – the "culture trap" excuse.

The culture trap is a state of mind that leads to sales paralysis on the part of those who fall victim to it. It is the idea that because, for example, the French are culturally distinctive from Americans, an American selling in France will suffer a crippling disadvantage. It is the idea that because, for another example, business cycles are longer/shorter in countries A/B, that a sales person from country C will be unable to adapt successfully.

I have no patience for this species of excuse, and for the simple reason that it overlooks one fundamental truth: The business process is universal, period. The "It's different here" or "That won't work here" contention is flatly wrong and ignores much of what we know to be true of human nature, of commerce, and of international relations in general. People generally want the same things, even if they get them in different ways.

If you ignore customs, you will at best stumble; at worst you will fail. But if you ignore business best practices, you will *surely* fail. Most successful businesses win because they have a good process. Process, in my experience, is international.

Imagine for a moment you have been in the business world for over twenty years. You now have an opportunity to walk onto the international stage. You step foot into your first international office on day one, you go to rollout what you believe is the winning plan, and someone says to you,

"That won't work here." If you're new to this world, you may find yourself scratching your head, wondering if this is correct.

What I will argue is that this is *partially* correct, but mostly false. What is non-negotiable when it comes to business anywhere in the world is the art of execution. In any business transaction, I would argue it is imperative that you get to the buyer most advantageously positioned to evaluate your product in relation to the larger business. This person will ideally have a budget. I also believe it is imperative that you understand the business impact of the solution you're selling. As much as I believe you must make dials to get people on the phone, I also believe you must talk to the people best positioned to understand your product in order to progress the sale.

I believe you must run effective, value-based sales meetings for the customer. I believe that without talking to the ultimate decision maker, you are 50% less likely to close a deal. I believe if you don't hold people accountable to their professional responsibilities, you will only achieve about 40% of your actual market potential. I believe in each of these factors, not one of which is unique to a specific culture; they are true in a global sense.

They are, however, greatly impacted and influenced by culture. In the U.S., I can easily pick up the phone, dial an executive, bypass other individuals lower in the chain of command, have a conversation about the impact of the business, and progress steadily through a normal sales cycle. In Japan, this may not be quite as simple. It does not mean you don't follow the same process, but it does mean you will go about achieving it in a slightly (sometimes dramatically) different way. In Japan, where hierarchy and respect are critical components of culture, it will take you longer to achieve the result you would more easily have achieved in the U.S. business. It might mean that what can be accomplished in two or three meetings in the U.S. will take you six or seven (or more) in the Japanese market. It might mean that while you can quickly gain trust and respect in one or two meetings in the U.S., it will take you perhaps months or even years in Japan.

There are ways to combat this, such as by hiring only local people in the market. You may decide that, instead of growing organically, you acquire a company that has a strong presence in the market, is more trusted in the country, and is therefore easier to maneuver within a specific market. Again, the key here is to not negotiate.

You know what is best, and you know how to run a business; it's imperative you do those things that lead to success. What you should do is work with local individuals in the market to build a plan of success utilizing your business background, fortified with their cultural knowledge and understanding, which collectively will enable everyone to achieve the end goal.

So, when you hear the phrase "That won't work here," push back and ask the question, "Do you believe this process does not work, or do you believe the way I'm recommending we go about achieving the process will not work?" It is likely the latter. If they say it is the former, then we must return to a lesson we talked about earlier in this book.

Remember when I said people tend to fail for one of a few reasons? They lack skill, they lack belief, or they lack ability. Remember, if they lack belief, it is your job to sell them. This is a prime example of an area where you must sell the employees on *why* this process ultimately *does* work.

When I was running Vietnam, I had a local managing director who presented me with this exact situation. I was trying to get this group to reach the executive level within their organizations, so as to better position our software products. I immediately received the pushback that this would not work in Vietnam. So, I asked the question of the day: Did they not believe going to the executives would work, or did they not believe in how I had recommended it?

The answer was, in fact, a little bit of both.

So I sold them on why the process worked, and then we agreed to do things their way as far as how we went about achieving the goal. On my next trip to Vietnam, I sat down with the managing director and asked how we were progressing with our strategy. He was hugely excited to share some of their recent successes. They had followed the agreed-upon process and the plan for achieving it. As a result, they had closed multiple new SaaS deals for considerably higher contract values than they had ever seen before.

This office and that managing director have continued to thrive in their market by following a business practice/*process* they had previously not used, one in which they originally did not believe.

Again, this goes back to what I am so earnestly trying to convey to the reader, which is that business processes are universal; culture is country-specific. Learning how to wed these two is ultimately the key to being successful in international markets.

Let's look again at Target.

Target did not fail because it did not recognize individual customs or cultural hallmarks. It failed because it moved away from its business best practices, those which made it successful for so many years in the U.S. market. The locations Target selected, which were based on an acquisition from a former Canadian retail chain, proved to be largely rundown and dumpy-looking stores in undesirable locations. This was a sharp contrast to Target's bright, shiny, clean stores enjoyed by consumers in the U.S. market.

Furthermore, because they went into Canada so quickly, they had huge problems keeping inventory on the shelves. Combined with the drab, depressing environment, Target's Canadian presence amounted to an unappealing shopping experience for the average consumer.

In the U.S. market, Target works by keeping its shopping experience "superior" to Walmart in terms of quality and selection. Because they were, in Canada, viewed as a low-end retailer, based on store locations and inventory constraints, they were forced to compete against Walmart, which had already been in the market for a long period of time and which offered lower prices. All these blunders resulted in Target's ignominious demise in Canada. These were not based on culture clashes or any legal misunderstandings. Target simply failed because they did not stay true to who they were. They were over-confident in their abilities and thus did not follow their own business best practices. The very practices that make them the successful retailer they are in the U.S. People in Canada undoubtedly went into these Target stores expecting good things. They did not get what they expected.

Focus (Revisited)

I told you earlier we'd come back to this. Only because it's important.

Products in international markets are generally localized, they renew at different rates from one country to the next, and they are not universally relevant. Organize your teams in such a way as to ensure they are able to maximize product renewal in the markets to which they are locally relevant. Keep your aim narrow and your quotas realistic. Don't try to turn every team into a Swiss Army Knife; that approach rarely works. Let them become masters of their products and of the selling of those products within markets receptive to them.

This sort of team/product/market alignment is essential to your success in a complex marketplace. For those of you with no interest in overseas selling, I advise this approach to your domestic sales strategy. Aligning teams with product-specific and geographically pertinent aims makes nothing but sense. It also makes money.

Those of you who have read this book in sequence know that focus is the foundation upon which my sales and leadership careers were both built. It is, more broadly, the bedrock of my personality. Without reiterating my earlier arguments, I will recalibrate them for a focus on international sales. And I'll start with this: To win the race, you run the race. Not five other races. This is easy to forget in a multi-national sales arena. There are so many irons in the fire at any moment, so many markets in which to sell, so many products to align with a given business's needs.

It adds up quickly, with focus being a common casualty of that accumulation.

My recommendation is that you initially identify three (no more) viable opportunities and allow them to dominate your attention. This goes for products, accounts, and markets. The "master of none" mentality can be hugely damaging to a sales career, particularly in a dynamic EMEA or APAC environment. You might try to achieve and exhibit high-level proficiency with, say, a half-dozen products/services, only to mistakenly advise a client in using the wrong one when asked for your "knowledgeable" input.

When I first arrived in the international markets, I realized a couple of things immediately: 1. We had everyone focused on every product, and 2. We were trying to sell every product in every market regardless of whether those products made sense for that market, were localized for the market, or even legal to sell in that market.

The foremost deficiency I addressed was focus. My belief is that nobody can excel in selling eight distinctive products. I think that if you have people siloed into specific product focus areas, those individuals will attain expertise both in selling that product, and within the industries pertinent to said product.

So, very quickly, what I did was to break up my sales force into product focus teams. In all these markets throughout Asia, nobody was having much success selling our new SaaS products. The simple reason for this was that they didn't *have* to be good at selling those products, as they could sell other products and still hit their quotas. The valuation on the products they were most often selling was 1/12 the value of the SaaS products we were attempting to sell.

We desperately needed to grow our software footprint in the Asian markets.

When we created teams that could only sell certain software products, those teams got very good at figuring out how to correctly position and sell those products within the Asian markets. Simply put, the only way they were going to feed their families was if they learned how to sell software...so they learned how to sell it, and well!

Now this next part is admittedly a bit of a restatement of Chapter VI, but I think it is a very critical point, so I do not mind taking the time to explain it again.

When I moved from Asia to the European markets, I quickly realized that in Asia, my focus on being focused just wasn't quite focused enough. I had gotten my people focused, but where I needed to further refine my approach was in product alignment. Europe, like Asia when I first arrived, did not have its people focused on specific business segments. One of the mistakes we made when launching into the international markets was that we took U.S. products and shoved them in, regardless of the market fit.

So, when I got to Europe, I quickly zeroed in on the problem. This time I started with a geographical matrix where I modeled out what products were sold by country, based on either existing architecture or my belief in our ability to deliver localized products in a reasonable amount of time. This meant that in every market, we eliminated some products from the total menu. It also helped us define very clearly our roadmaps for those products we were continuing to sell.

The way I achieved this was simple. I met with my leadership team and told them they had one week to come back to me with three products we would sell going forward. Everything else would be eliminated or moved to "sustain" mode. We then debated and ultimately settled on the right products for each country. Once I clearly understood the actual product matrix we would be moving forward with, we aligned people and product, providing focus for the sales teams.

I also initiated the hunter/farmer methodology, which provided additional focus. I wanted new logos coming in the door, and I wanted to maximize customer value. It's hard to be truly good at both without focus, so we split up the teams to accomplish these goals. Again, this was met with some resistance—but in the end, it proved to be successful. New logos went up, retention went up, and overall customer value climbed.

Revenue grew steadily with selling focus on the right products. It is a great case study on how important market-specific product focus is for a successful international strategy.

Likewise, you might look at the whole of Asia as fertile ground for your sales efforts, but fail to recognize which countries are most likely to need or benefit from what you have to offer. When you find yourself spread too thinly, the work of responsibly withdrawing into a more manageable strategy can prove costly, time-consuming, and embarrassing.

As I have previously stated, "Just because you can make money at something doesn't mean you should." I've run my business in accordance with those words for over ten years' time. And I've been right to do so.

I think it's worth talking about a major issue I found with product fit by market. One of our SaaS offerings was a terrible fit for one specific European country. Without getting into too many details, we had no business selling this product in that country. The problem was that prior leadership believed this U.S. product should be sold throughout Europe, without regard for many of the things we have already covered. At first glance, you would have concluded this product had achieved moderate success. They had sold around 120 units by that point, accounting for a fair amount of revenue.

The problem was that leadership had basically told the employees to sell 100 units in the calendar year or risk being fired (a threat they could not legally have carried out, anyway!). Whether they turned a blind eye, didn't know, or didn't care, I will never know. But for the sales teams to get to the 100 units, a shell game ensued. They went to customers with an absurd proposition along the lines of, "Hey, you bought this product last year. Buy this new shiny thing this year and I will give you the product you bought last year for free." The contract's value was baked entirely into the one product that did not (and could not) work. It was essentially useless to the customer.

This slippery sales maneuver might have worked if the customer had, you know, implemented and used the new SaaS product. But they did not. In fact, most did not use it even once. A few tried it out, but with no success. We found many others who literally had no idea they had purchased it. This created all manner of issues by renewal time. We had customers telling us they did not want the new SaaS in their contract, which, because the products they liked and used were now valued at zero or at a highly discounted rate, made renewals very difficult to negotiate. We literally went to zero revenue for that SaaS product, by the way.

Let's review what we've covered so far: 1. Understand that sales is a universal human phenomenon, not the sole domain of any one country; 2. Acknowledge cultural differences, but don't be paralyzed by them. Business is business; 3. Focus your time and energy intelligently. You must be discriminating in the allocation of limited resources.

Understood?

Okay, with those concepts now firmly rooted in your mind, let's talk a bit about organization.

I have discussed alignment earlier in the book and cannot overstate its value. To read in one chapter about what I spent four years doing throughout Europe and Asia is to only skim the surface. What I can tell you is that in markets where I had alignment with the local Managing Director, my teams all enjoyed tremendous success. In markets where I did not have that alignment, the teams struggled. This was a bigger issue in Asia, probably because I was new to these challenges and had the wool pulled over my eyes more easily. Nowadays, lack of alignment will exclude a Managing Director from being a part of my team.

I do not tolerate lip service, contradictory behavior, or dishonesty. In those markets where alignment was an issue, those Managing Directors were moved out of the business. That is not to generalize Asia as a whole. I had several extraordinary Directors with whom I was grateful to have worked. These individuals continue to experience extraordinary success in their respective businesses.

In Europe, I was blessed with a group of great leaders. Alignment was not a problem. Initially there was some pushback, but this is always to be expected. We quickly established rapport/trust and, as a result, achieved incredible results.

Key to effective alignment is clear communication. Without it, the aligning process may fail to take shape effectively. Make sure every subordinate leader, every sales rep, every support tech, and even the office maintenance crew is aware of what each team is responsible for, and what each team is *not* responsible for. Clarity is golden. Once the team knows what to do and knows they have your express blessing in doing it, the work can get underway unhindered.

Provide detail in spades and leave nothing to any rep's imagination. To whom are we selling? What are we expected to sell? How much are we expected to sell? Why are we being thusly aligned? Make sure you answer each of these in thorough detail. You will run the risk of repeating yourself. So, repeat yourself. They will thank you for as much, at least tacitly, once your vision is realized.

American sales professionals are accustomed to being hit with radical change. They take a second or two to let the change register, and then they execute, often without understanding the details, the larger goals, and so on. In my international experience, the opposite was the case. They demand to know everything. So, take advantage of that. Use it as an opportunity to elaborate on blueprints which often go unexplored in United States sales shops.

Now, this next bit will be a bit daunting for some of you. Steel yourselves.

Communication must move down <u>and up</u> the ladder. This has never been a challenge for me. When I have committed to a certain team/product/market alignment, I make it known to my bosses...immediately and plainly. I leave no room for uncertainty in their minds. For my teams to function as I know they should, they need to be unhindered by interference from the top brass. Said brass will be less likely to interfere if they know why I am doing what I am doing. This often (very often) means delivering big truth pills to senior figures who don't always like what I have to say.

But they do respect me for saying it.

The result is that the sales professionals I am charged with making more productive...

...end up being more productive. I purchase them the latitude necessary to ensure that they can function as they need to, and then let my investment accumulate interest. It's a reliable formula, one that will also work for you. But you must be willing to make your case up the hierarchy. I still marvel at the number of "tough" sales leaders who become sheep when in the presence of someone higher up the corporate food chain. Remember: It's easy to be a tiger when surrounded by those obligated to play the part of lambs. It's far more difficult to maintain that image when the power differential is not in your favor—it is also never more essential and respectable.

As for the strategy underlying your alignment blueprint, it must be constructed with care, executed with diligence, and inspected often. Note: Adding headcount rarely qualifies as a strategy. It can be a strategic move, but it does not on its own deliver increased revenue if your overarching sales formula is rubbish, nor if the product you are selling is of lower quality. At most, you might enjoy a year of revenue growth; but this will be followed by two years of migraines brought on by lost business, not to mention the expense of installing support structures to manage your unsustainably burgeoned revenues.

To be clear, alignment is a process. It is the process of communicating your vision, gaining buy-in for that vision, establishing agreed-upon metrics by which subordinates will be measured and to which they will be held accountable, then constantly checking and inspecting to ensure there are no cracks in the dam.

When you combine focus and alignment, you can create the business equivalent of magic!

Sundry Observations and Thoughts

For cultural reasons, American businesses—certainly their sales departments—operate with the unstated notion that ½ equals one. There's something very American about the idea of rounding up. Kentucky windage, in other words, has its equivalent in the world of U.S. sales.

There is no such thing as German windage.

In Germany, only one number equals one. I'll give you two guesses. Okay, it's one. Period. Beyond accounting, spreadsheets, and pricing, your products must also adhere to the "one equals one" precept.

The German business world is a graveyard of failed American attempts to make inroads.

Laws differ drastically from one country to the next. Sweden is a good example, as women there are entitled to maternity leave amounting to a year or more. Men receive half as much for paternity leave and are permitted to gift all or some of that total to their wives. Managing around such considerations can prove challenging. The bottom line is that it pays to know the local employment laws, the rights of its citizens, and how these can impact your business.

Back to the remarkable economic powerhouse that is Germany, wherein an employee with at least six months' time on the payroll cannot be fired by an employer. Consider that for a moment. They cannot be fired by their employer. In effect, they must agree to be terminated, and under conditions of their choosing. As mentioned earlier in the book, nascent cultures tend to emphasize citizens' responsibilities; plateaued cultures tend to emphasize citizens' rights. That is a major distinction, one with enormous implications for private sector employers.

One key area where this can be costly is in an acquisition.

Imagine you plan to purchase a German company. You may be thinking you will acquire and then right-size the business, or simply acquire the intellectual property, but not the employees. While you could easily do this in the U.S., this might come at great expense unless you place the burden of said expense onto the seller. Food for thought.

Offhand comment: France is essentially a cultural/legal hybrid of Germany and Sweden, though perhaps with better cuisine. You can terminate people, but there are regulations around what is owed to an employee based on years of service. Again, check on this with your local legal advisor.

The concept of vacation in Europe differs from its American counterpart in several crucial ways. Vacationing professionals do not answer phone calls while away, nor do they respond to emails. Aside from the fact that this likely suits the vacationer just fine, the law happens to be on their side. Yes, there exist actual laws which prohibit those on holiday from seeing to business matters until they have returned to work. In France, such restrictions have been made to include evenings and weekends. The separation between professional and personal time is very real in Europe, alien though the concept is to virtually any American reader.

This is an ideal place to make plain the fact that European professionals are not inherently lazy. There are lazy Europeans, of course, but on balance they are a highly productive bunch. I would confidently place the aggregate of their work ethic against its American counterpart any day of the week. The outcome might come as a surprise to you. My French office was submitting contracts at 10:00 P.M. one evening. That evening, I might add, was New Year's Eve. Says a lot.

Regardless of where an international assignment may send you, my best piece of advice is to GO! It will be incredibly rewarding. You will undoubtedly make mistakes. If you are lucky, you will meet some amazing people. And you most surely will see the world through a different lens. I could write an entire book on just this alone, but we are running out of time, so I need to move on now.

Chapter X:
Startups, Turnarounds, and High Growth.

ALMOST EVERYTHING IS CYCLICAL to some extent. I know that's a huge generalization, but there's truth to it. The business world is a good example. An idea turns into a startup, a startup turns into an ascendant business, an ascendant business turns into a thriving enterprise, a thriving enterprise turns into a decadent behemoth...and the decadent behemoth inevitably begins its downward spiral, until it is either acquired or forced into a merger or acquisition. And somehow the wealth it accumulated along the way finds itself into a startup's coffers via investments and the like, which keeps the cycle going.

The historian Will Durant put it simply: "A nation is born a stoic and dies an epicurean." What this basically means is that when a country (or business) is young, its pioneers are strong in spirit, frugal in expenditures, creative in thinking, and willing to suffer as necessary. When a country (or business) begins to decline, its people seek pleasure, comfort—both of which were made possible by earlier generations. Once the bank account runs dry, those epicureans lack the know-how (and what we Texans call grit) to turn things around.

There's a point to all this: Wherever you find yourself in the lifecycle of a business, you owe it to yourself and to

169

those you lead to do good work. If your sales career lasts as long as mine has, you will probably find yourself working for a startup, for an industry juggernaut, for a mid-sized company, and for a declining operation at various points. There are financial benefits and plenty of perks to working for a juggernaut, of course. But there are character-building benefits to keeping a sinking ship afloat. Your expense account might be limited, but you'll learn to do more with less.

Let's tie this philosophy in with some of my own experiences.

It was my first leadership meeting as a newly appointed Area Sales Manager. Partway through, a man got up in the front of the room and announced that the company was giving accounts from an inside account team back to the field offices managed by this group of leaders. It was further explained that since they did not know where the accounts stood, we would be getting the accounts, in bulk, at approximately 25 cents on the dollar. Upon receiving our account lists, it became immediately clear that my own was by far the largest in terms of contract size and overall number. When looking at the expiration dates, I learned that, unfortunately, all save one were inactive.

I was new and a little confused, so I leaned over to one of the more tenured leaders and asked if I was correctly analyzing the data. He analyzed the list, handed it back to me, then mumbled "You got screwed.".

Almost immediately, the man in the front of the room, who happened to be the company CEO at that time, spun around. His narrow eyes, slightly squinted, were directed straight at me. He walked with purpose to within a foot of where I sat. Literally everyone around me, including the guy who made the comment, slid their chairs away from my own, leaving me exposed and vulnerable. It was not unlike the parting of the Red Sea.

What happened next was one of the most impressive F-word barrages I've ever witnessed. The CEO leaned over me, index finger extended at my face. I leaned back, trying to create some separation, but he just leaned in closer. "What the f#%* did you say? Are you F#%*ing kidding me? If you cant F#%*ing do something with those accounts, you are in the wrong F#%*ing job. Why don't you shut your F#%*ing mouth and do your F#%*ing job? In fact, maybe you should just F#%*ing leave now. Are you F#%*ing kidding me? You are un-F#%*ing real. You will never F#%*ing be successful here with that F#%*ing attitude. F#%* ME!" The room was dead quiet. I wanted to crawl under anything I could find, but there was nothing to hide under—everything and everyone had abandoned me by that point. I did not respond. I just sat there, stunned, freaked out, and pissed at the idiot who made the comment, only to let me take the lashing.

As it turns out, the CEO became one of the people I most admired in my career. He was a wicked smart business guy. He had a temper, but he was good. Really good. A few years later, I asked him over dinner if he remembered that story. He said he did not remember, but went on to say, "I don't know what happened, but all I can tell you is that I love you now.". It was literally the most amazing compliment I have received in my life. That should give you an idea of the admiration I feel for this man.

One of the interesting things about leadership is that in your career, if you're lucky, you will have the opportunity to lead multiple types of businesses and learn from some incredible people.

I have led in many of the business cycles I mapped out above.

I have found myself in a start-up environment in which we essentially grew from nothing. I've had the unequaled pleasure of working in a rapidly ascendant company that grew from $36M to almost $800M over six years' time. I have undergone extreme turnaround situations and have led in an organization after it was purchased by one of the largest private equity companies in the world.

All these situations are unique…and all of them require a different set of skills. Yet they also require that you remain faithful to your values, the values that have either propelled you to success or will soon do so.

The man referenced above has voiced some great business quotes in his day. One of these is: "If you run your business like you are in trouble, you never will be.". This remains some of the best advice I have ever received. At its core, it argues that you should never rest on your laurels. When things are tough, it's easy to work hard, spend wisely, move with urgency. When things are great, to the point of seeming as though losing is impossible, you can grow lazy, soft, turn a blind eye to the "push-ups" and "sit-ups" of the job. This is dangerous and sees many great companies eventually falter.

In 2008, the company in which I held a senior leadership position had been on an amazing growth trajectory when we were suddenly faced with the reality of the Great Recession. As growth slowed, we started to put more focus on activity. I had not pulled a dial report in years, but decided one day to do exactly that, probably out of sheer frustration with the numbers.

I was shocked.

The report showed that the highest number of dials by a single rep that month was eighty. The lowest was twelve! *Twelve* calls for one month, that's barely one call for every two business days. Are you kidding? The minimum for a week when I used to really manage down to that level was 250. Remember the spinning plate example from earlier? I had forgotten to spin the dialing plate. As you can imagine, with so few dials, we also had few appointments. With few appointments, we had fewer deals, lower revenue...you get the idea.

The wise man with the amazing ability for utilizing one of my favorite four-letter words had another quote. He often said, "Activity is always the problem, but it's never the answer.". In this case, it was definitely the problem, but it would not get us out of the larger economic trouble with which we had been confronted.

Activity is just one driver of success. Activity alone will not get the job done.

During the recession we were forced, like many companies, to execute a round of layoffs. That was a tough time. The worst part is that our product was tied directly to employment; thus, the Recession hit us particularly hard. And unlike Wall Street, we were not in line for a government bailout.

We became hyper-focused on the business during this time. We buttoned up the activity problem. In fact, we told people that provided they were doing the push-ups/sit-ups of the daily job requirements, their jobs would not be in jeopardy regardless of performance. We worked hard during that time. We trained our people on better selling/closing techniques. We focused intently on niche opportunities within industries. We bundled our products differently and grew close to our customers.

The last of these was central to how I ran my zone.

It was during this time that I launched the C-level initiative I mentioned earlier. In one of my favorite books, titled *Managing by Influence*, the author writes about the fact that you can put a cricket in an old coffee can and put the lid on it. The cricket will try repeatedly to jump out, thumping itself against the lid. Eventually, the cricket will give up. It will simply stop jumping. When this happens, you can remove the lid without risking the cricket making an escape—it will sit there and die.

I had previously tried to reach the C-suite, but was unsuccessful. That did not mean I planned to sit in the bottom of the can and die. I knew C-levels everywhere were in the exact place I was at the time. They would listen to anything if they thought it could help them grow, save them money, or both.

I devised the aforementioned plan, set out to execute that plan, and did so with amazing success. It allowed us to change the conversation, move upstream, and secure larger deal sizes.

Life is about windows of opportunity. If you decide not to jump when the window opens, you will miss out on opportunity. But if you have the foresight and the guts to jump, the rewards can be exceptional. I took advantage of this window at that time and achieved amazing success.

Our largest and most aggressive competitor declined by more than 25% in 2009. We declined by around 5%. This was still tough, as we had been growing by double digits for months, quarters, years. Nonetheless, I believe our relative stability was remarkable in and of itself. It certainly ran counter to most industry predictions.

Another of my favorite quotes: "Spend the company's money like it is your money.". Again, words to live by for any executive, leader, or aspiring leader. In a startup you want to create, grow, be big, go public or sell, make millions, buy a private jet, and live the good life. Finite is the number of people who end up achieving that.

You would think that even though an entrepreneur's money really is theirs, they would know this, but many have egos and, by extension, a desire to be validated—to be a real company. To them, being a real company means having a sign, nice office space, a receptionist, a ping-pong table, top of the line computers, courtside seats, sitting in business class, driving a nice car, etc.

I cannot stress how important it is to resist such urges. Every dollar you direct to unnecessary expenses is a dollar that cannot be spent on necessary ones. When starting out, it takes time to achieve the financial success needed for that desirable exit outcome. Most entrepreneurs under-estimate the savings they will need in order to start making money. In this world, being fiscally responsible is critical. Keeping costs to a minimum will buy you more time...valuable time. Time to learn, to grow, to ultimately succeed.

In larger companies, it is easy to make poor spending decisions. You may buy airplane tickets and stay in hotels based on, say, your preferred rewards program rather than on the best deal. You may choose flights based on schedule rather than price. You may choose lavish dinners instead of moderate or good dinners (the clients usually don't care). You might plan a trip to see one client instead of trying to book multiple meetings around the anchored meeting to maximize return. The list of the wasteful goes on...and on...and on.

At the end of the day, companies exist to maximize shareholder value. Private equity understands this concept *very* well. They are masters at trimming corporate fat. They look at everything. They will put teams of people on expenses looking into things like, for instance, vendor consolidation. They apply discounting pressure onto existing vendors via procurement. They implement Deal Desk, ensuring all pricing going out to customers is not in the hands of the sales reps, but rather controlled to ensure optimal profit margins per deal. They look into things like span of control. Essentially understanding the average number of employees per manager by level, and by technical scope. In doing so, they will cut out costly leaders. Not all of them, but definitely some of them. When beginning, they may find averages of three to four employees per manager. By the time they are done, they will have moved these averages up to eight to ten in some areas; fifteen to twenty in others. Such savings are meaningful.

They will review things like SLAs to see if a company is doing more than they are contractually obligated to do. If so, they will either stop performing those tasks or start charging for as much after discussing it with the customer. They review implementation costs to ensure they are being passed on to the customer, and that they also meet the set profit margin minimums. They look at every segment in a company and ensure they are profitable. If they cannot get them there, they remove people from the business until they can do so. They take control of travel and entertainment budgets. They restrict flights to only pre-approved travel that meet certain criteria.

They also push for innovation. They typically bring aboard strong leadership in different functional areas to move the company forward. They draw from their years of business experience in multiple industries and bring in knowledge experts. These individuals can have a shocking impact on improving finance, ops, sales, technology, product, and marketing.

Private equity is in the business of making money for its shareholders. Going through an acquisition by a PE firm falls well short of fun. You must make a lot of tough choices to achieve what they expect of you. The fact is, these PE firms are successful because companies are largely fiscally irresponsible. Maybe they grew quickly and simply felt they didn't need to be that frugal.

Perhaps they just didn't know what they didn't know.

Regardless, PE firms buy on the cheap, work their magic, and squeeze every penny of EBITDA (earnings before interest, taxes, depreciation, and amortization) they can out of the company, increase the market value, and sell for large increases above their initial investment; or they keep the now-leaner organization and pass on those yearly returns to their shareholders.

I have also worked in organizations that we wanted to sell. If you find yourself in this situation, I can save you some time and money (and make you a lot) by recommending you simply re-read the last few paragraphs and apply those best practices from private equity. There are exceptions, but a company that generates $100M in revenue while losing $50M is worth $0, or at least a lot less than a company that makes money. The likelihood of your being one of those exceptions is not very high. Companies like Uber are said to lose billions every year, yet still carry mind-blowing valuations. So, if you are Uber-esque, spend away. Everybody else, pay attention.

When you start a business, it's almost always with the hope of selling. Your sales price will be derived from many factors, including EBITDA, revenue, growth rates, retention rates, market conditions, type of product, strategic positioning for a potential buyer, and a variety of other things. EBITDA is what determines their ability to recoup their investment. Higher EBITDA = higher sales price. Now that is a basic explanation, but it is also a fact. The SaaS world has examples of companies that are revenue-driven valuations, but again, a higher EBITDA will raise the multiple on the revenue side.

As such, controlling your costs like a PE firm will deliver meaningful increases in value for your company.

So where does this tie in directly to sales leadership?

Okay, pay attention.

No matter where the company stands, how much cash it has on hand, how much headcount it needs to add or cut, how many competitors it has overtaken or been overtaken by, your job is your job—to grow revenue. That's true in a startup with one day of operations to its credit, and that is true of a dying behemoth with one day separating it from bankruptcy.

Your job...

...is...

...to...

...grow revenue.

There will be different challenges with each phase of the business lifecycle; I acknowledge that. Everybody should.

In fact, the challenges with a wealthy company often come from within. I'm not talking about bloated entertainment budgets. I'm talking about internal competition. If you're the only game in town (and this never lasts long; ask McDonald's), the challenge might be keeping choice accounts from being siphoned to a rival office. It might be preventing your top dogs from getting promoted too early (as discussed earlier in the book). It might be keeping prices from getting out of control. It might be preventing your reps from getting too cocky...which always happens in a thriving company. The reps often lose sight of how much they are benefiting from marketplace considerations that have nothing to do with their sales prowess.

So, those are a few challenges to consider when you are leading in a hyper-prosperous company. Only a few—that list could easily go on.

A company just beginning to decline is another problem entirely. Suddenly, reps who had counted on easily making the President's Club (while spending stupid amounts of company money on airfare, dinner, et cetera) are having to actually, you know, work. And the response is always disproportionate, trust me. A minor dip in marketplace strength results in a huge dip in sales rep morale. This is mostly due to that entitled (or epicurean) mindset.

"I've always made the President's Club with ease. What the hell is going on? My quota is unfair. My manager does not know what she is doing. This company sucks."

Yes, loyalty purchased with a buck is easy to lose. A company in decline will see the mercenary types jumping ship within months. As a leader, you have to account for that. Who are you likely to lose? Who will stay and, more importantly, *why* are they staying? Is it the job security? Do they still believe in the company? Do they believe in you? Figure that out quickly.

Your next job is to determine how the company is actually performing. Is there a chance of a full recovery? Are the good times ever coming back? Will the company fail within five years? You need to know these things for your own sake, but you also need to know what to tell your team. You also need to know what to tell potential new hires. Even sinking ships continue to bring people aboard.

A company nearly ready to breathe its last breath...

...take a moment to think on that idea.

Okay, this is a weird situation for any employee, but sales leaders in particular. First of all, why did you stay so long? Are you close with the CEO? Were you promised a "golden parachute" for the trouble of sticking around to turn the lights out?

If you know the answers to those questions and are at peace with them, then you can turn your attention to where it belongs. The last remaining reps will want to know what's happening, and when. Be honest. If possible, set them up with jobs elsewhere. Sales is a musical chairs profession. Make sure none of your reps are still standing when the music stops.

And by the way, keep bringing in revenue. Until the doors are chained up or your paychecks have stopped clearing, you have a job to do. An NFL team might be down four touchdowns in the final minutes of the game, but they owe respectable play to themselves and to the fans. Set a good example. You will find employment elsewhere. Make sure the reputation that follows you is that of the leader who led well; both when money fell from the sky and when it dried up entirely.

To summarize, we cannot always choose the circumstances in which we lead. Those circumstances surround us, and we react accordingly. How we react is important. A nation might have reached its epicurean phase, but that does not mean every citizen must behave like an epicurean. Be a stoic throughout your career. And try to experience sales leadership in every phase of the company lifecycle. Just make sure you have some savings set aside while working for a startup or for a declining business. Which reminds me—save a lot while working for a behemoth. I mean *a lot.* This occupation is basically a roller coaster. Thick and thin...thick and thin.

Be a stoic every day.

A final note on this topic—your teams will always deserve as much candor as you can provide. Don't bullshit them. If the company is about to take a downward turn, let them know. If their success is largely owed to the company selling an awesome product with no real competition around, tell them that. If they are doing good work under bad circumstances, praise them. If they are doing bad work under bad circumstances, do not praise them.

Let truth be your touchstone.

And, seriously, spend at least a year working for a nose-diving company. The lessons you'll learn are priceless.

Chapter XI: A Summary & Some Final Words

BREATHE.

If you read this in the time it took you to fly from one coast to the other...breathe. I've thrown a lot at you.

Here's the bottom line: Establish a few principles for yourself and stick to them. You'll find that strong sales leadership principles will carry over into other parts of your life. Accountability, gathering knowledge, honesty, loyalty—these will also serve you well as a sales leader, as I have argued, but they will absolutely serve you well in your larger life. So, hold yourself to them and improve your overall daily existence while also achieving your sales quota(s).

Control

You've got to know what you can control and what you can't. If the economy is tanking and your business is taking a hit, that is not fun. But unless you're running the Federal Reserve, there's not a lot you can personally do about that.

What you can do is continue to hold your team accountable. You can make sure activity doesn't decline. You can adjust your sales strategy. You can even argue up the chain, if necessary. In fact, let's get to that right now.

Know When to Fight

I'm a fighter. If you're not a fighter, you may need to rethink your career goals. I just mentioned arguing up the chain. What I mean is that there will be times when you have to go to bat for your team, your office, your territory, et cetera. Now, if you've earned credibility and rapport with the senior leadership, you'll have a lot more success in defending your people. Earning that credibility requires being good at your job, being consistent, being selfless, and being fearless.

Maybe quotas need to be adjusted while the market is nose-diving. Maybe your zone lost a handful of great accounts to the corporate office, leaving your top reps in a bad spot. Maybe pricing needs to be reined in. I can't tell you what sort of case you'll need to make, but you will need to make one at some point. Make sure you have enough standing in the organization to do so without being laughed out of the room.

Be strong enough to fight and credible enough to win. And don't waste your asks on petty things. Make sure they are the ones you are willing to die on the hill for. Most importantly, make sure your supporting information is correct. There is nothing worse than being wrong about an ask of large magnitude.

Understand Your Talent

Knowing who you have on "the field" is just as important in a sales office as it is in the NFL. Even an average football coach will have a strong understanding of what strengths/weaknesses characterize each player. Perhaps your most athletically gifted running back is least willing to suffer for the team. Maybe your slowest receiver will bleed himself dry for a touchdown. To lead well, you've got to know what each player (sales rep) can do on the field (on the phone).

And please remember what I said about acknowledging good work and calling out poor performances.

I'll reiterate.

There are reps and young leaders I've loved like family (or at least close friends) who have fallen short of their potential. I am the first one to call them out. Sometimes it's that rep who should easily be at 180% YTD but is just barely sitting at 100%. Other times it's the rep who could be at 100% if they had followed the plan, but can't seem to break 95%. No matter the case, if they aren't where they should be, I don't care how frequently we've hung out in our off-time—I'll make sure they know they're doing awful work.

On the other side of the coin, there are some reps I barely knew at all from a personal standpoint. Reps I had nothing in common with. You know what? When they hit their quota, brought in a big deal, or just plain surpassed my expectations, I always made sure they were recognized. It's the right thing to do, and it just might earn you some loyalty from unlikely sources.

The point here is don't just focus on your favorites. It's a human weakness to do exactly that. But as a leader, your job is to be objective. Evaluate based on performance; don't get too caught up in the socializing aspect until business is taken care of. And you never know whose day you might make by directing some unexpected praise their way. Do what's right.

Keep a Long View

Everybody in sales and/or sales leadership is guilty of it: We all find ourselves thinking from quarter to quarter. Hell, even financial industry titans with decades in their business will occasionally have trouble looking beyond whatever three-month timeframe they're operating in at the moment.

You've got to take a longer view.

There will be times when your company is running away with it. No competitors in sight, customers itching for more of what you're selling, money growing on trees. But those times can't last. You need to look ahead one, two...five years—you need to make sure your sales reps are ready to deal with competitors, ready to chase customers rather than simply take orders, ready for a potential drop in income.

This doesn't obligate you to behave like a pessimist. You don't need to adopt a naysaying mentality. Just remember that business is cyclical. There are patterns and predictable changes. There are also the *unpredictable* changes...and these are rarely for the better. Enjoy good times while they last, but plan well for the inevitable change.

And remember, the opposite is also true. Bad times are also temporary. Your reps might be tempted to panic when a competitor enters the marketplace with lower prices, superior technology, better branding, or just the benefit of being shiny and new. Even your own leadership will be prone to overcorrecting in the face of serious challenges— slashing prices too quickly, rushing untested products to market, hastily adding or eliminating headcount.

Through it all, try to keep a long view. Remember your principles. Be honest with both your reps and your leaders.

And allow loyalty its due. When times are good, your sales reputation will thrive. The headhunters will come calling. They might present you with a tremendous offer, one you might consider. Do that—consider it. But don't jump at *every* tremendous offer. I would never suggest you hitch your wagon (career) to one horse (company), but there is something to be said for giving each employer at least a couple of years. It'll allow you to dig in to the product/service they're selling, really learn it up and down. Plus, you might come away from those two years with meaningful, lasting friendships and business relationships. Bouncing around from one company to another might be worthwhile in a short-term, "get the cash while you can" context. But it might not serve you well in terms of building up a solid career foundation.

Anyway, take or leave that advice. Our career experiences are all unique.

Get In the Trenches

Leadership is complex. It generally comes with certain privileges. Privileges first create a feeling of comfort, then a feeling of entitlement. Not in every case, but that does happen.

For your part, never regard leadership as anything other than a responsibility. The privileges may be there...in fact, they almost certainly will be there. Fine. That doesn't have to create a feeling of entitlement. When you feel anything like that beginning to manifest, get yourself back into the trenches. Go on sales meetings, sit in the row with your team, host a miniature account review session—something, anything to keep the comfort from compromising your integrity.

Now, earning a leadership role is tough. I can tell you that firsthand. And keeping a leadership role, well that's something else entirely.

I am not here to cheapen that fact. If you've worked hard to get where you are, I'm proud of you. I really am. You should enjoy the fruits of your labor. Just enjoy them on your own time. As for business hours, those belong to your team; they do not belong to you. Give your team everything you can. Teach them, guide them, demand they work as hard you do, and make sure they get the credit when things go right.

Look, when you're taking your second flight to the Caribbean in eight months' time, you can savor every minute of your hard-earned success. And believe me, it's worth the wait. We all like the idea of being treated like aristocracy.

Some companies regard their leaders as something like minor royalty. I'm telling you, that's the wrong way to go. It'll alienate your team and, in the end, cripple your sales capacity.

Get yourself in the trenches. You won't be making tons of dials, I get that. But you should be in front of clients. You should be at each rep's side at least once or twice each week. Research your competitors, research your industry, research all technologies relevant to your business. Leadership is not a recliner; it is a driver's seat. Drive.

Candor

If I had limited myself to writing about only one topic, it would have been candor. Honesty, more generally.

I can't place enough emphasis on this. Candor is the essential leadership ingredient. Yes, hard work is important. Knowledge is important. Trust and loyalty are important. Objectivity is important.

You know what? None of these amount to anything if you are not direct and honest with everyone in your professional life. As I stated earlier, being plainly candid with your reps is one thing, being plainly candid with your own leaders is another.

There's an adage that goes something like, "A true test of character is how you treat people who can do nothing for you." I might modify that for corporate leadership: "A true test of character is how honest you are with people who can fire you on the spot."

I've known plenty of people who can talk tough to lower-ranking employees, but quickly become yes-men when in the presence of corporate brass. Whatever mistakes I've made in life or in leadership, one thing I am not is inconsistent. You're as likely to see me coming down hard on a poorly performing sales rep as speaking hard truths to my boss's boss.

There is risk in that approach. The reward is credibility and respect. If you are correct in what you are saying, the person to whom you are speaking will almost always recognize that fact. Some will ignore the truth, but most will not.

This philosophy might be contrary to your personality. It is the nature of many people to be highly deferential in the presence of the powerful individuals. That's just fine. Show them respect and expect they will do the same for you. But don't withhold truthful statements out of fear of being punished. Aside from the reality that people tend to detect insincerity pretty easily, the facts will always come out eventually anyway. You may as well be ahead of them.

My reputation is one of being candid at all times with all people. Earlier in my sales leadership career, this characteristic came across more negatively than I intended. Many reps thought I was unnecessarily harsh. I've acknowledged that.

The overall trajectory, however, has seen me earning the trust and respect of people at all levels by being consistent. I've come down hard on reps and on peers, yes. I've also spoken my mind to the C-suite and to top-dollar clients when the situation called for it. This doesn't mean I'm out there picking fights.

Not at all.

But I do have my principles. Being candid at all times is one of them. If that principle sees me ramming heads with higher ranking individuals, I honor the principle. If it sees me telling an underperforming rep to stop placing blame elsewhere, I honor the principle.

I honor the principle.

～～～

You know my thoughts on advice. Most of it isn't worth the time it takes to hear.

Feel free to ignore this advice.

Learn every day. Don't think for a moment that you know it all. And learn from every person you encounter. Even the newest rep on your team has at least two decades of life experience unique to them. You have no idea what they do and don't know. Learn from them.

Fail in a big way at least once, and then take a handful of important lessons from the struggle that follows.

Get to know different people throughout the company. Perhaps you work in sales on the sixth floor while IT operates on the fourth. Go make inroads. Introduce yourself; take an interest in what they do. Being a leader means knowing a lot more than what's in your lane.

Take a chance on a hire here and there, but otherwise play that bit safe. Yes, even a "sure thing" can end up quitting in three weeks while the "long-shot" retires from the company twenty years later. More often, though, your gut and your sense of what your team really needs will serve you well. Still...take a chance once in a while. Remember the zipper salesman?

Make plenty of time for your family or, if you are single, for yourself. A sales job at any level can easily dominate your life. When you're on the golf course, consider turning off your cell phone. When you're at the kid's baseball game, leave it in the car.

There may be times when you are living for the job. That's all right when you're under thirty. Once in your thirties, remember that life is short. And if you're already in your forties, I hope reading this book was a good use of your time.

Above all, do right by your team. Leadership, as I have said, is a responsibility. Lead well.

Last, enjoy the journey. I hope yours is as rewarding as mine has been.

That'll do it. At least until the next book...

-Will Emmons

www.ingramcontent.com/pod-product-compliance
Lightning Source LLC
Chambersburg PA
CBHW060552200326
41521CB00007B/559